W9-BKM-049

Ferdinand Magellan

RACHEL A. KOESTLER-GRACK

GREAT EXPLORERS

Jacques Cartier

James Cook

Hernán Cortés

Sir Francis Drake

Vasco da Gama

Sir Edmund Hillary

Robert de La Salle

Lewis and Clark

Ferdinand Magellan

Sir Ernest Shackleton

Ferdinand Magellan

RACHEL A. KOESTLER-GRACK

GREAT EXPLORERS: FERDINAND MAGELLAN

Chelsea House
An imprint of Infobase Publishing
132 West 31st Street
New York NY 10001

Library of Congress Cataloging-in-Publication Data
Koestler-Grack, Rachel A., 1973-
Ferdinand Magellan / by Rachel A. Koestler-Grack.
p. cm. — (Great explorers)
Includes bibliographical references and index.
ISBN 978-1-60413-422-3 (hardcover : alk. paper) 1. Magalhães, Fernão de, d. 1521—Juvenile literature. 2. Magalhães, Fernão de, d. 1521—Travel—Juvenile literature. 3. Explorers--Portugal--Biography—Juvenile literature. 4. Voyages around the world—Juvenile literature. 5. Discoveries in geography—Juvenile literature. [1. Magellan, Ferdinand, d. 1521.] I. Title. II. Series.
G286.M2K73 2009
910.4'1—dc22 2009011587

Chelsea House books are available at special discounts when purchased in bulk quantities for businesses, associations, institutions, or sales promotions. Please call our Special Sales Department in New York at (212) 967-8800 or (800) 322-8755.

You can find Chelsea House on the World Wide Web at http://www.chelseahouse.com

Series design by Lina Farinella
Cover design by Keith Trego

Printed in the United States of America

Bang EJB 10 9 8 7 6 5 4 3 2 1

This book is printed on acid-free paper.

CONTENTS

Mutiny!

The voyage along the Patagonian coast of Argentina had been hard on the Spanish fleet and the sailors. More than once, the ships had barely missed being driven aground on dangerous reefs. Every vessel had been battered by relentless storms and was in bad shape. Ferdinand Magellan's fleet set sail from San Lúcar, Spain, on September 20, 1519. About 260 men were aboard the five ships, and all of them were cold and discouraged. Some crewmen believed Magellan would lead them all to their deaths. They grumbled constantly about how they should just return to Spain. Some of the Castilian officers provoked the discontent and dissention. They did not trust Magellan and wanted to see him fail.

Magellan knew that quitting was not an option, not for him at least. If he returned to Spain without reaching the Spice Islands, his future would be shattered. Someone else would be chosen to lead the next expedition, and he would be thrown in jail for having deceived King Charles I, the ruler of Spain. At

During the fifteenth and sixteenth centuries, Spain and Portugal—both superpowers—were in competition to claim and settle newly discovered regions of the Americas and the East. The two countries split the globe in half from pole to pole, with some of the Spice Islands remaining unexplored. After Magellan's plan to gain access to the Spice Islands failed to win support from Portuguese king Manuel, he got approval from Spanish king Charles.

the very least, he would be utterly humiliated. He was determined to continue his mission, no matter what hardships lay ahead. Magellan assured the men that they would not starve or freeze. There was plenty of fish and shellfish, as well as wild game on shore. By spring, the ships would be ready to sail for the Spice Islands. Furthermore, he pointed out how the men of Castile were famous for their toughness, courage, and resourcefulness. How would it look to the world if a few snowflakes scared them so much they had to run back to Spain? The fleet anchored in a bay Magellan named San Julián to wait out the winter.

Many of the crewmen may have been stirred by Magellan's words. Still, the Castilian high command loathed him and would not budge from their position. They were sick of the dangerous coast, with its devilish storms and icy blasts. They were willing to do anything to get back to Spain before it was too late. They spread rumors throughout the crews that Magellan had made an alternate plan with King Manuel of Portugal. They said that he had sworn to his former king that he would destroy the fleet by wrecking most of the ships and marooning the survivors. After he made it back to Spain, he would inform the king that there was no westward passage—news that would thrill Portugal and discourage Spain from sending out another expedition. Their lies stirred suspicion among some of the crewmen. Juan de Cartagena, who resented serving under a Portuguese leader, spread the thickest of the lies. Cartagena also had not forgiven Magellan for placing him under arrest while the fleet was off the coast of Africa. Together with Captain Gaspar de Quesada of the *Concepción*, Captain Luis de Mendoza of the *Victoria*, and some of the officers from all three ships, Cartagena devised a scheme to overthrow Magellan.

On the night of April 1, 1520, a boat from the *Concepción* carrying Quesada, Cartagena, and 30 armed men pulled silently alongside the *San Antonio*. Álvaro de Mesquita, newly named captain of the *San Antonio* and a cousin of Magellan's, and most of the crew were sound asleep. The ship was only lightly guarded. When the armed men climbed aboard, the guards did not have time to sound an alarm. Quesada and Cartagena marched directly to Mesquita's cabin. With swords drawn, they burst through the door, grabbed him out of a dead sleep, and dragged him on deck. The rest of the armed men had already herded the rest of the sleepy, bewildered crew on deck. Quesada reminded the crew members of the unnecessary hardship Magellan had inflicted on them. He explained to the mainly Spanish crew that under a Castilian command (instead of a Portuguese one) the men would no longer be mistreated. He then asked the crew of the *San Antonio* to help restore proper authority to the fleet and join a mutiny against Captain-General Magellan.

The loyal Mesquita flatly refused to have anything to do with a revolt against Magellan. The mutineers bound Mesquita in shackles and locked him in one of the cabins below deck. Suddenly, the shipmaster, Juan de Elorriaga—who was also loyal to Magellan—awakened by the ruckus, rushed on deck. Apparently, the mutineers had forgotten to check his cabin. As soon as he found out that Captain Mesquita had been taken captive, he confronted Quesada. "I demand, in the name of God and King Charles, that you return to your ship!" he snarled. "This is not the time to be going among the ships with armed men. I also demand that you release our captain!" Enraged, Quesada pulled out his dagger and plunged it into Elorriaga, stabbing him six times. Seeing their shipmaster sprawled in a pool of blood, there was no further opposition from the crew.

Quesada took over as captain of the *San Antonio*. Cartagena took command of the *Concepción*. With Captain Luis de

Mendoza on the *Victoria*, three of the fleet's five ships now were controlled by the mutineers. Meanwhile, on the two other ships, the *Trinidad*—the flagship—and the *Santiago*, no one knew what was happening.

Early the next morning, Magellan sent a small crew from the *Trinidad* over to the *San Antonio* to pick up four men and go ashore. As the skiff approached, a sailor on the *San Antonio* warned them about what had taken place the night before. The men quickly rowed back to the flagship and told their commander the alarming news. The little *Santiago* was anchored alongside the *Trinidad* near the exit of the bay. No one onboard was yet aware of the mutiny. The men aboard the *Trinidad's* skiff rowed up and asked Captain Juan Rodríguez Serrano, commander of the *Santiago*, if he pledged his allegiance to Magellan. Puzzled, the captain quickly answered yes.

Later in the day, the longboat from the *San Antonio* brought Magellan a message. It listed all the grievances of the mutineers. In addition, the message stated that Quesada, Mendoza, and Cartagena had seized the three ships to make sure Magellan would take them seriously. If he promised to meet their demands, they promised to acknowledge his leadership and release the ships. Magellan sent the messengers back with a note of his own. He invited the three captains to come to his ship to discuss the issues properly. If they did, Magellan promised to hear them out. A little while later, the longboat returned to the *Trinidad* with a response. "We don't dare board your ship," the message said, "for fear of mistreatment." Instead, they proposed the meeting take place on the *San Antonio*. Magellan decided that he would give them no more time to organize their plans. He set a counterattack in motion.

At dusk, Magellan summoned his master-at-arms, the tough, reliable Gómez de Espinosa. He sent Espinosa and one of his marines, both armed with concealed daggers, to hand deliver a message to Captain Mendoza on the *Victoria*. At first, Mendoza refused to let them aboard. But Espinosa taunted him, asking him if the noble captain was afraid of an unarmed messenger. Finally, Mendoza allowed the two men to board the *Victoria*. Mendoza escorted the two men to his cabin where he read over Magellan's message. As he read it, a smile spread across his face. Before long, Mendoza roared with laughter. Apparently, Magellan's letter suggested something ridiculous. Just then, Espinosa grabbed the captain by the hair, yanked his head back, and thrust his dagger into Mendoza's exposed throat.

Meanwhile, Duarte Barbosa, Magellan's brother-in-law, and 15 heavily armed men had silently rowed the longboat along the *Victoria*. Suddenly, they swarmed aboard and quickly disarmed the startled watchmen. The rest of the crew offered no opposition, and the *Victoria* was back under Magellan's command. Espinosa shouted, "Long live the Emperor and death to traitors!" The mutineers aboard the *San Antonio* and the *Concepción*, however, were sound asleep and had no idea their plan had been foiled. During the night, the *Victoria* was brought up next to the *Trinidad*. The *Santiago* and the *Victoria* floated on either side of the flagship, blocking any exit to the sea by the *San Antonio* and the *Concepción*. The mutinous ships were trapped.

The next morning, the mutineers realized that the tables had turned against them. They released Mesquita and begged him to plead with Magellan to show mercy on them. Mesquita refused, telling them it would be useless anyway. Their only hope was to slip past the other three ships guarding the harbor entrance. They would wait until darkness and try a desperate escape. Even under the cover of night, it was impossible to make their move without alerting the *Trinidad*. The thump of ground tackle and the rustle of canvas gave them away.

In the moonlight, the watchmen on the *Trinidad* clearly saw that the *San Antonio's* sails had been hoisted and its gun ports opened.

Magellan prepared his flagship for combat. To win the men's cooperation, he also allowed them an abundance of food. Meanwhile, Magellan had a special assignment for one of his seamen. He was to sneak onto Quesada's ship, *Concepción*, and loosen or sever the anchor cable so that the ship would drift toward the blockade guarding the mouth of the harbor.

As soon as the *Concepción* came alongside the *Trinidad*, Magellan ordered the gunners to fire rounds of heavy shot into the *Concepción's* hull. When the *Concepción* drifted close enough, an armed party scrambled on deck. "For whom do you stand?" they shouted at the crew. "For King Charles and for Magellan!" they promptly responded. Magellan then dispatched a party to take over the *San Antonio*. The men onboard pledged their allegiance to Magellan and handed over the mutinous Cartagena. He was taken to the *Trinidad*, where he was shackled below deck with Quesada and the other conspirators. The expedition to the Spice Islands would go ahead as planned, and Magellan proved he would not let anyone stand in his way.

Famous by Chance

Today, Magellan is famous for leading the expedition that made the first circumnavigation of the globe. Yet, he had never actually dreamed about sailing around the world—or, if he did, no one knew about it. In the plans he submitted to King Charles, he made no mention of such a goal. His objectives were to find a westward route to the treasured Spice Islands and to prove they were part of the Spanish empire. In fact, he had said if he could not find a westerly route, he would return to Spain. He failed in both of his objectives. If he had made it to the Spice Islands, he probably would have chosen the same route of his

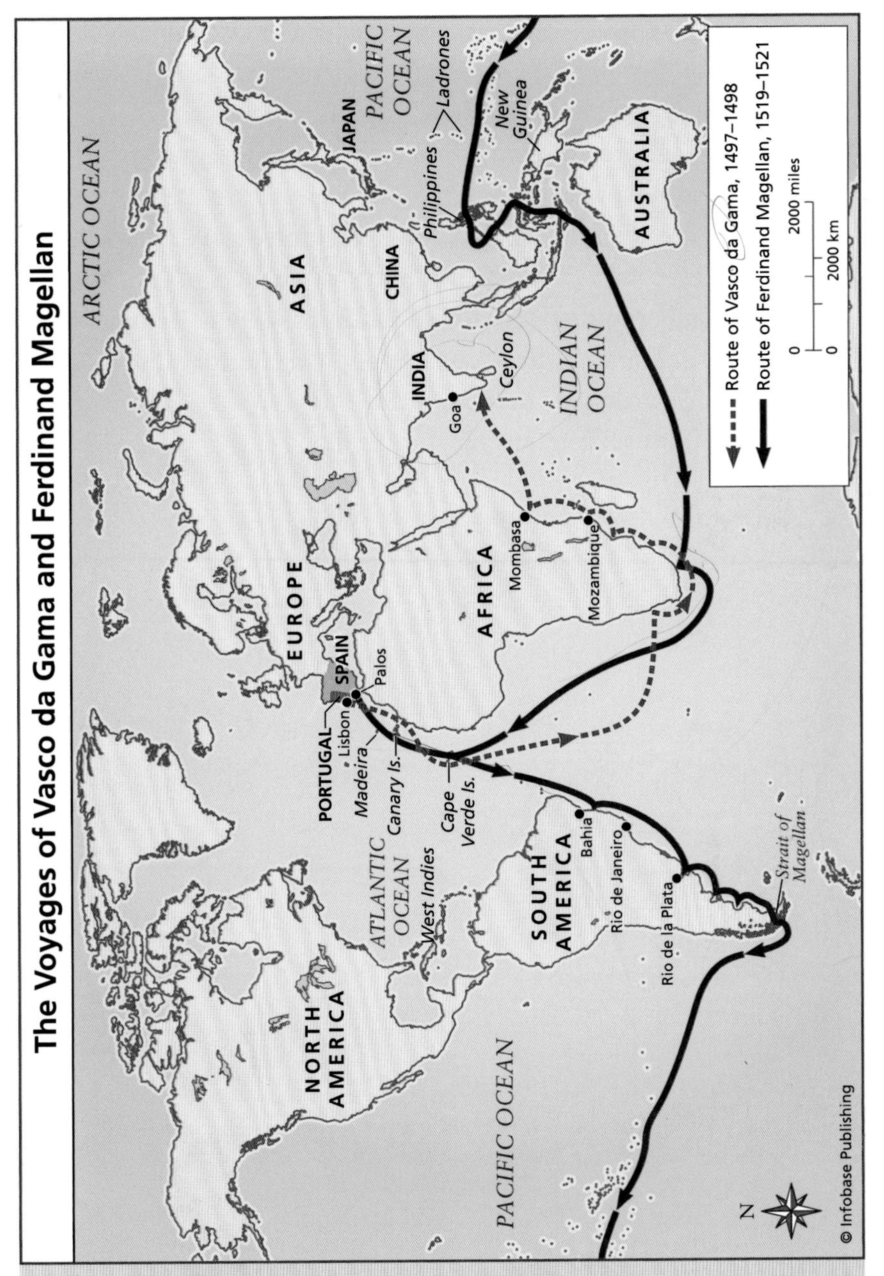

Vasco da Gama's discovery of a sea route to Asia gave Portugal control of the lucrative spice trade, leading to its rise as a world power. With four ships, he rounded the Cape of Good Hope, passed the easternmost point reached by Bartholomew Diaz in 1488, continued up the east coast of Africa, and sailed across the Indian Ocean to Calicut. Da Gama's successful journey set the stage for Magellan's epic voyage around the world.

one remaining ship—the *Victoria*. The idea of circumnavigating the world would have merely been a practical choice. It was the best way to get the fleet home from the Spice Islands.

Nevertheless, the world will never know how Magellan felt about being called a circumnavigator. He died in the bloody Battle of Mactan that took place on April 27, 1521, in the Philippines. He became famous by chance, not for the political and economic goals he had envisioned. Rather, it was the circumnavigation, completed by a mutineer he had grudgingly pardoned, that captured the imagination of the world and future generations.

Maritime Masters

THE EXACT TIME AND PLACE ARE UNKNOWN, BUT BETWEEN 1470 and 1480 the future great sea navigator Ferdinand Magellan (Fernão de Magalhães) was born to Rodrigo de Magalhães and Alda de Mesquita. As a young boy, he lived in Nobrega, a part of northwestern Portugal along the Lima River. Ferdinand was a descendant of an adventurous French Crusader who fought in the Iberian wars of Duke Eudes (Odo) of Burgundy toward the end of the eleventh century. His father was a sheriff of the port of Aveiro—an honorary position awarded to him for his distinguished service to the king.

At the age of seven, Ferdinand joined his older brother, Diogo, at school, probably at the neighboring monastery of Vila nova de Muia. Magellan's parents died when he was 10. Two years later, he followed his brother and became a page to Queen Leonora in Lisbon. As an attendant to a member of the noble family living at the castle, Magellan took his first step toward becoming a knight in medieval society. Queen

Leonora was the wife of King John the Perfect, who had held the Portuguese throne for 12 eventful years. At this time, education for most Portuguese children was limited. Children at the royal courts, however, were taught reading and writing, religion, arithmetic, music and dancing, horsemanship, and martial skills. In Lisbon, they also took courses in algebra, geometry, astronomy, and navigation. At an early age, Ferdinand's schoolwork focused on nautical studies. He was being trained for life at sea, a trade for which Portugal became famous. Some historians believe he was taught by navigator and geographer Martin Henhaim.

Although the country was small and rather poor, Portugal had led the way in the area of exploration. The Portuguese proved to be masters of maritime adventures. In 1488, under King John, Portuguese explorer Bartholomew Diaz sailed around the Cape of Good Hope, a rocky shoreline on the Atlantic coast of South Africa—farther than any other European sailor had ventured before. He pressed on all the way around the southern tip of Africa. Not long after, Pedro da Covilhã—whom King John had assigned to find cinnamon and other spices in the Near East by way of the Mediterranean Sea—explored the mystical land of India. Afterward, he crossed to the eastern coast of Africa and voyaged far south to Sofala.

Despite these incredible feats, Spain began stealing the wind from Portugal's sails. About this time, Christopher Columbus, from Genoa in Italy, had first gone to King John to present his plans to sail westward to the Indies. With Diaz's successful rounding of the southern tip of Africa, an eastern route was under Portugal's control, and the king was no longer interested in funding a western route. After traveling to Genoa and Venice and not finding encouragement there, Columbus gained the support of the king and queen of Spain. Despite the great explorations of the Portuguese, the voyage of Columbus was the one that would spark the imaginations of Europeans.

The Age of Exploration (fifteenth to seventeenth century), also known as the Age of Discovery, was a period during which Europeans explored the world by ocean in order to gain riches, knowledge, and power. The first great wave of ocean voyages was launched by Portugal, and soon after Castile (present-day Spain) became major competition in the quest for new trade routes and colonies. The map above is bound by four major explorers (*from upper left*): Christopher Columbus, Amerigo Vespucci, Ferdinand Magellan, and Francisco Pizarro.

His discovery of America (which at this time Columbus believed was part of Asia) opened the astonishing possibilities about what might lay beyond the ends of the world.

Young Ferdinand, an awestruck page in the Portuguese queen's court, may have even seen the great discoverer. In March 1493, on his return trip to Spain, stormy weather forced Columbus to bring his ship *Nina* into the Tagus River, where he anchored off Belém, Portugal, near Lisbon. When King John learned that Columbus was off the Portugal coast, he at once invited the explorer to visit him at the monastery of Santa Maria. There, Columbus proudly told the king of his discoveries. On the way back to Lisbon, Columbus passed through the village of Castanheira, where the queen was staying at the convent of San Antonio. Columbus stopped at the convent to pay his respects to her highness on his way through town. Although no one knows for sure, Ferdinand quite possibly could have been there that afternoon, standing wide-eyed in the courtyard as Columbus dismounted his mule. Whether or not young Ferdinand actually laid eyes on the famous

THE AGE OF EXPLORATION

The desire to explore unknown, faraway lands has been a driving force in human history since the dawn of time. Since the beginning, ancient civilizations have explored the earth by sea. Early adventurers were motivated by religious beliefs, the desire for conquest, the need to establish trade routes, and a hunger for gold and riches.

The Age of Exploration, also known as the Age of Discovery, was a period in history that stretched from the early 1400s through the early 1600s. During this era, Europeans explored the world by ocean in search of new lands and goods for trading. The most desired trading goods were gold, silver, and exotic and rare spices. Europeans used new sailing ship technologies to find a trade route to Asia. The most important developments were the Portuguese creation of the carrack and caravel ship designs. These vessels were the first ships that could leave the relatively calm waters of the seafarer, he certainly heard the news of Columbus's astonishing voyage to the New World.

Undoubtedly, King John was devastated by Columbus's successful venture, especially because he had found the idea ridiculous several years earlier. Up until this point, Portuguese ships had ruled the high seas. Now, Spain had found a western route that was even more promising than any the Portuguese had ever made to the south or to the east. At the same time, Spain had stumbled upon lands previously unknown.

Race to Rule the Sea

After King Manuel took the throne in 1496, Portugal maritime superiority began to be challenged by Spain. With such an impressive rival, Manuel felt pressured to set out additional

Mediterranean, Baltic, and North seas and sail safely on the rugged, open Atlantic Ocean.

The first great wave of expeditions was launched by Portugal under Prince Henry the Navigator in the early 1400s. Venturing into the open seas, expeditions under Prince Henry led to the discovery and settlement of the Madeira and the Azores Islands. Henry the Navigator's primary target was exploration of the west coast of Africa. For centuries, the only trade routes linking West Africa with the Mediterranean world were over the western Sahara Desert. These routes were controlled by the Muslim states of North Africa, long rivals to Portugal and Spain. Prince Henry hoped to bypass the Islamic nations and trade directly with West Africa by sea.

Within two decades of Portuguese exploration, the barrier of the Sahara had been overcome and trade in slaves and gold began in present-day Senegal. In 1487, Bartholomew Diaz made a crucial breakthrough by rounding the Cape of Good Hope, proving that ships could reach the Indian Ocean by way of the Atlantic Ocean. Then, in 1498, Vasco da Gama used this route to reach India, setting the stage for Ferdinand Magellan's epic voyage around the world.

expeditions. As of yet, no one knew just where Columbus had landed. In fact, up until his death in 1506, Columbus still believed his discovery had some direct link to Asia. Still, the Spaniards had not found any spices in this new land—cinnamon, nutmeg, pepper, or cloves. Most explorers at the time were concerned about discovering these valuable spices. Both Spain and Portugal knew that these spices did exist in the Indies—the lands the Portuguese hoped to reach by sailing around the distant Cape of Good Hope. Portugal was determined to win the race to rule the sea.

By July 1497, four Portuguese ships were ready to set sail for the Indies. King Manuel chose Vasco da Gama to command a new expedition to India. As da Gama's fleet set sail, Portuguese hopes and expectations soared. No European had yet made his way by sea to the lands beyond the Cape of Good Hope. The voyage would be riddled with dangers. The distance alone seemed immeasurable. Even to reach the Cape of Good Hope, the ships would have to sail for months over treacherous seas. The distance from the cape to the land that Pedro da Covilhã had visited was almost as great. In fact, in comparison, the voyage of Columbus was much shorter and less perilous.

Da Gama did not return until September 1499. Only two of the four ships and a third of the crew survived the 26-month expedition. Yet it was one of the greatest voyages ever completed. There was no doubt that this expedition was ranked equally with that of Columbus—only this time the Portuguese took the fame, reclaiming their throne as rulers and heroes of the sea.

Although 17-year-old Magellan longed to be part of a great voyage, he was not yet interested in leaving his position at court to serve as an apprentice explorer. In 1502, da Gama, now admiral of India, set sail on a second voyage. A year later, Alphonso de Albuquerque sailed for the Far East. Again, Magellan stayed behind. In 1505, Dom Francisco de Almeida was appointed to serve for three years as the first viceroy of Portuguese India. He was authorized to lead a powerful fleet to that faraway land. Finally, at 25, Magellan enlisted in the fleet.

Although Magellan had seen and spoken to respected commanders, he had no hands-on experience with the sea. As a child, he had grown up in the rugged uplands of the Traz-os-Montes e Alto Duro (Beyond the Mountains and Upper Douro), far away from the Atlantic Ocean. At court, his duties gave him little time to spend on ships. White-capped waters were part of his heritage, however. For centuries, the Portuguese have been seafaring people. Even though he grew up farther inland, he most likely picked up some nautical knowledge along the way.

The voyage to India would certainly bring adventure and possible fame, but Ferdinand was hesitant to leave behind the life he had known for the past 12 years at court. He understood that shipboard life meant hardships and grueling work. He was careful not to resign from his position at court, because he might want to return to it. Instead, he asked for a leave of absence. In this way, he could enlist as a *sobresaliente*—a supernumerary—a temporary employee without authority and with few specific duties. As the fleet set sail, however, destiny was about to unfold before him. He could not have possibly imagined what lay ahead in those murky waves.

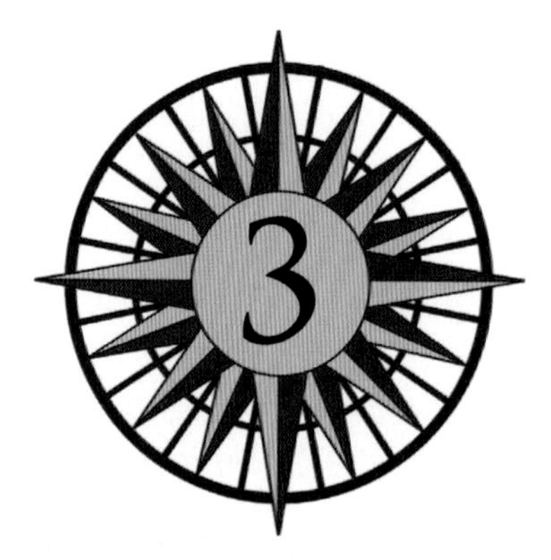

The Voyage to India

On March 25, 1505, Magellan sailed for India with a fleet of 22 ships under the command of Francisco de Almeida. Almeida was being sent by the king to be a permanent representative in the East. Besides the ships' crews, Almeida's fleet carried 1,500 soldiers, 400 artillerymen, and a group of supernumeraries—a conglomeration of adventurers who could perform both civil and military duties. Among the supernumeraries were Ferdinand, his elder brother Diogo, and his cousin Francisco Serrão. As the ships pulled out of the harbor, the majestic crash of cymbals and the brave blast of trumpets slowly faded away. The tide in the river turned toward the rushing sea, and the music was replaced by the sound of sails whipping in the wind and the harsh slaps of waves beating the sides of the vessels. It was a noble mission, to face the ruthless seas on a voyage to India. But Magellan, like the others, knew that danger awaited them. In the earliest voyage to India, led by Vasco da Gama, only two of his four ships returned, bringing

Magellan's first voyage at sea was when he joined Francisco de Almeida's expedition to India in 1505. Almeida *(above)* and his crew of 1,000 plus 1,500 soldiers were sent by King Manuel to bring the spice trade under Portuguese control, to construct forts along the East African and Indian coasts, to gain alliances with local leaders, and to build trading posts. His victory in the battle of Diu signaled the beginning of Portuguese supremacy in the Indian Ocean.

back a feeble third of the men who had gone along. On the second expedition—that of Pedro Álvares Cabral in 1500 four caravels and all the men onboard were lost in a sudden storm in the South Atlantic.

Soon, the men came face to face with the awesome power of the Atlantic Ocean. As the squadron swiftly sailed along with the southerly winds, a tempest suddenly arose. A torrent of rain came down in heavy sheets, the wind needling it against the sailors' faces. The heaving waves tossed the ships back and forth like little toys, tipping the flagship—the *San Miguel*—so far on its side that the yardarms touched the sea. Many of the sailors thought they were doomed. They dropped to their knees and shouted prayers to the heavens, weeping in despair. Just at that moment, brilliant, sputtering balls of fire appeared at each masthead, blinding the men with their bright orange glow. The superstitious sailors shouted for joy, believing their prayers had been answered. The blazing orbs were a sign from the saints, telling them they were saved. Actually, what they were seeing was a natural electric phenomenon common on ships with high masts, known as St. Elmo's Fire. But to these mariners, it was a miracle, which was at once confirmed. Just as quickly as the storm had hit, the violent winds calmed.

During another gale, a gray albatross appeared in the sky. It hovered almost motionless over the *San Miguel.* No one aboard had ever seen such a creature. They had only heard about the bird in the dreadful stories of superstitious captains. The albatross was often believed to bring a deadly curse on a ship. As the men watched in frozen silence, the albatross circled in the air, soaring without the slightest flap of it wings. All of a sudden, two more birds appeared, one of which was black, terrifying the sailors even more. Their fears were soon lifted, however. The winds died down and the ominous birds flew off into the mist.

Although his observations showed their position on the chart to be at 35° south latitude—well below the Cape of Good Hope, located on the Atlantic coast of South Africa—the chief pilot, Pero Anes, continued to hold his southerly course. On their own quests, both Bartholomew Diaz and Vasco da Gama had turned back at this point. Still, Anes announced that the squadron would push to 40° south latitude—or several hundred miles farther south beyond the cape, before doubling back toward the Indian Ocean. This path was common of Portuguese navigators who were too worried to risk the wild waters of the cape. They would rather travel hundreds of miles out of the way, exposing the men to the frigid zone of Antarctic winter, than risk themselves and their crew in the hazardous currents around the cape.

The Antarctic waters are known for their enormous waves suddenly shifting winds, and raging storms. They are perilous even for modern-day vessels. In 1505, as Almeida's expedition rounded the Cape of Good Hope, the pilots were blindly navigating through unknown waters. On June 20, three months after leaving Lisbon, Almeida's fleet finally rounded the cape. Still, they were not in safe waters. In that region, warm currents from Cape Agulhas clash with the frigid Antarctic stream, causing violent storms. At the end of June, a hurricane formed, beating the vessels with alternating blasts of rain, hail, and snow. The turbulent waves tossed the ships with incredible strength. At one point, the wind ripped the sails completely off one of the ships and spun the vessel like a cork in the whirling sea. Waves swept across the deck, carrying three crewmen overboard. At daybreak, the skies finally cleared. By some miracle, one man was still swimming in the icy water and was rescued. Day after day, the weather became milder, and soon the fleet moved into the calm waters of the Indian Ocean.

After rounding the Cape of Good Hope, Almeida's fleet sailed northward along Africa's east coast, at last anchoring off the Primeiras Islands. Here, a ship carrying a detachment of soldiers was sent to reinforce the garrison at Mozambique, about 200 miles (321 kilometers) to the northeast. Meanwhile, Almeida continued north with eight warships, while the slower merchant vessels sailed directly to India. Magellan's name did not appear on the records until more than a year after Almeida's fleet arrived in East Africa, so there is no way to know for sure whether Magellan sailed with Almeida's warships or the merchant vessels. Nevertheless, it was during this period that Magellan began to emerge out of the shadows and into history's spotlight.

On July 22, Almeida arrived at the port of Kilwa on the East African coast. He overthrew the hostile sheik who was in power there and replaced him with a rival who swore loyalty to the Portuguese king. Then, the soldiers built a Portuguese fort at Kilwa and assigned a military unit to defend it. From Kilwa, the fleet pushed on to Mombasa, a coastal port further north in Kenya. Again, the ruling sheik would not bow to Almeida's demands, so the soldiers torched the city. Next, Almeida sailed across the Arabian Sea, anchoring briefly at the Angediva Islands—off India's Malabar Coast—to build a fort there. Finally on October 21, 1505, Almeida arrived at Cannanore and formally declared himself viceroy of India. He later transferred the city of authority to Cochin because it was easier to defend.

That fall, loaded with spices and other trade goods, the annual flotilla—a small fleet of warships—left for Portugal, sailing from Cochin with the northeast monsoon. Seeing the departure of the flotilla, the ruler of Calicut and his Egyptian allies planned a surprise attack on the remaining Portuguese warships. An Italian traveler—Lodovico di Varthema—alerted the Portuguese of the plot. Almeida's oldest son, Lorenzo, led a Portuguese squadron to halt the Egyptian attack off Cananore. During the bloody skirmish, Francisco

Serrão fought valiantly and was later honored for his bravery. Although little is mentioned about Magellan's part in the fight, he was listed among the casualties—his first battle wound. The Portuguese won the battle.

In November 1506, Almeida ordered Captain Nuno Vaz Pereira to sail to East Africa with supplies and reinforcements for the fortress at Sofala. Apparently, Magellan had earned the respect of his commander, because Almeida assigned him as one of the captains aboard the bergantim. This large, oar-propelled, flat-bottomed boat was used for ferrying troops and supplies along a coast. From Sofala, Pereira returned to India in September 1507, on the ship *Sao Simao*. Magellan and his cousin Serrão were among the young officers he took along.

More than two years had passed since Almeida's powerful fleet had first sailed up the Malabar Coast. In this time, much had been accomplished. Forts had been built, cities had been captured, commercial treaties had been signed, and a victory had been gained at Cannanore. Almeida's son had proved to be an effective leader, not only in battle, but he had also rounded the southern tip of India. No European had ventured into these waters since Marco Polo had passed through on his way to China in the mid-1200s. Almeida's son Lorenzo had actually visited Ceylon (present-day Sri Lanka) and established a settlement there.

After the victory at Cannanore, no Egyptian or Indian had dared to rebel against the Portuguese. However, up and down the coast, from Quilon in the south to Diu in the north, opposition was growing. To make tensions worse, the Portuguese had so heavily interfered with India's trade in the Red Sea that even the wealthy of Egypt was suffering economically. At last, the sultan of Egypt was forced to send a fleet of warships to the coast of India. At the mouth of the Indus River—1,000 miles (1609 kilometers) north of Cochin—the fleet was joined by a convoy of Arab and Indian vessels, ready to take revenge on their Portuguese enemies. Meanwhile, after hearing about the impending attack, Lorenzo headed north toward the Arab coast in search of the Egyptian-Indian fleet. Near Chaul, just south of what is today Mumbai, Lorenzo's ships were caught off guard by the enemy. The Venetian gunners on the Egyptian ships brutally riddled the Portuguese ships. After two days of ferocious fighting, the Portuguese lost 140 men, including Lorenzo. Suffering the loss of their leader, they were forced to make a hasty retreat. The Egyptian-Indian forces had won the battle, but they had unleashed a Portuguese temper that hungered for vengeance.

Almeida was enraged by the loss of his son and the humiliating defeat of the Portuguese squadron. On December 12, 1508, he set sail in pursuit of the Egyptian-Indian fleet with 20 warships. Magellan was an officer aboard one of these ships. He caught up with some of the enemy ships at Dabul (currently known as Dabhol). Immediately, Almeida ordered his men to bombard the fortress that protected the harbor. The attack quickly drove the surprised defenders out of the city. Almeida personally led an army of soldiers on land to scale the city walls. The soldiers destroyed the walls and towers and set the town ablaze. No one was spared. The Portuguese soldiers slaughtered men, women, and children. The massacre was so terrible, from that day forward, the Arabs often spoke this curse: "May the wrath of the Portuguese fall upon you as it did on Dabul."

Again at sea, the Portuguese soon met up with the Egyptians near the harbor of Diu, which was the headquarters of the fleet of the great Indian king of Cambaya. The battle of Diu took place on February 2, 1509. During a long-distance artillery encounter, Almeida inflicted heavy damage on the Egyptian fleet. Shortly after midday, the Portuguese fleet closed in on the Egyptians. Captain Pereira led his men onto the deck of the Egyptian flagship while Almeida's *San Miguel* pulled up along the opposite side, also unloading its men. Magellan, part of Pereira's crew, followed his captain on board. After a bloody fight, the Egyptian ship finally fell to the Portuguese. Disheartened by the loss of the flagship, the remainder of the Egyptian fleet tried to retreat. Only several of their ships managed to escape.

For the Portuguese, the battle of Diu was a historical event. The victory ensured control of Asian waters and led to the collapse of the Egyptian Empire. However, the triumph came at a price. Captain Pereira lay dead upon the deck of the Egyptian flagship, and in the jumbled mass of lifeless bodies, Ferdinand Magellan lay critically wounded. For many days, Magellan fought to stay alive, and it took him many months to recover.

Malacca

In India, Magellan earned a reputation as a brave and noble man. In July, Magellan and Serrão signed on for an expedition to Malacca, commanded by Diogo Lopes de Sequeira. Almeida had heard rumors that the Spaniards were seeking a westward route to the Spice Islands. He desperately wanted to get to this coveted area first. King Manuel I realized that Malacca was the key to controlling trade from the Spice Islands to markets in India and Europe. He urged Almeida to establish a base at Malacca before Spain had a chance to do so.

In September 1509, Portuguese captain Garcia de Sousa's ships anchored off Malacca. The appearance of armed Portuguese vessels sparked concern among the Arab merchants there. They knew the Portuguese hoped to break the Arab-Venetian monopoly in the spice trade, not to mention the ferocity with which they attacked all who opposed them. The merchants treated the Portuguese courteously, but with great caution. On the third day after their arrival, Sequeira sent a Portuguese delegation to the sultan of Malacca. The two sides drafted a peace treaty, and the Portuguese were granted permission to open a trading post near the waterfront. Charmed by the

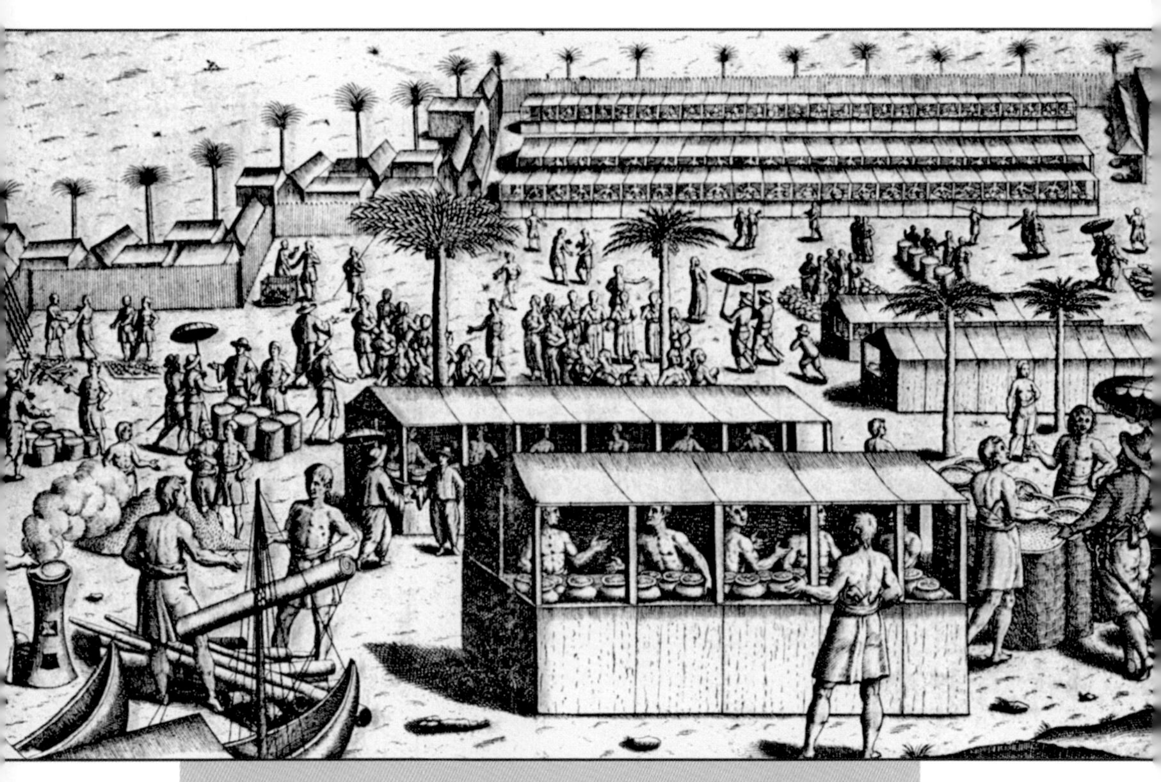

Malacca became a major trading center because of its position along the East-West trading route on the Strait of Malacca. The monsoon winds enabled Arab and Indian traders from the West to travel to China in the East and vice versa, and Malacca soon became a major player in the spice trade. At the height of its power, the country comprised modern-day Malaysia, Singapore, and a large part of eastern Sumatra, Indonesia.

apparent goodwill of the sultan, Sequeira requested permission to begin trading immediately so that he could load his ships in time to sail before the end of the southeast monsoon. The sultan kindly agreed. In addition, he offered to trade a large quantity of pepper he had stored in a warehouse some distance from the waterfront. He asked Sequeira to provide a group of men to transport it to the pier.

Some Chinese merchants tried to warn Sequeira that it was a trap. Eager to get the pepper, Sequeira ignored their warnings and sent 100 men to the warehouse. A friendly native girl also warned Serrão that it was an ambush, but having been selected to lead the party, Magellan's cousin chose to go

SPICES

At the time of Magellan's return to Lisbon, Portugal had become quite wealthy. Portuguese vessels regularly brought spices and other goods from the Far East. These items were more valuable than anything Spanish explorers, like Columbus, had found in the New World. Before the Portuguese discovered the route to India, the spice-trade monopoly had been in the hands of the merchant princes of Venice and Genoa on one side and the Muslim traders of the Indian Ocean and the Red Sea on the other. Through brute force, the Portuguese broke this spice ring and gained considerable control in the region.

Today, it is difficult to imagine how spices could play such an important role in a country's economic status. In Magellan's day, there was little variety in the types of food people ate. Most meals were dull and flavorless. Potatoes, tomatoes, and Indian corn were all native to America. Europeans had not yet tasted these foods. Tea and coffee, though widely served in Asia, were not part of the European diet before the 1500s. Only fruits and vegetables that could be dried were available year round, and because refrigerators had not yet been invented, fish and meat could be preserved only when they were dried, smoked, or salted.

Any spices that could offer seasoning and zest were hard to come by. Salt, honey, and a few dried herbs were available, but sugar was scarce and costly. For centuries, people had known that a little pepper, or a sprinkle of ground mustard, ginger, or cinnamon, would turn an ordinary meal into a scrumptious feast. Therefore, there was a great demand for

(Continues)

(Continued)

these spices, but they were found only in the Far East. Until the Portuguese reached India, the shipment of spice from certain parts of the Far East to Europe had always been a slow and costly business. When the Portuguese took control of the spice trade, the prices of these items dropped, allowing more people to purchase them. However, the Portuguese quickly established a monopoly of their own—long before Spain began profiting from the wealth of the New World. At this time, Portugal was well on its way to being the richest nation in Europe.

anyway. The warnings proved to be true. The sultan planned to trap the transport party at the warehouse while an army seized the weakly defended ships. As Serrão's men headed inland, a fleet of sampans infiltrated the Portuguese ships, pretending that they wanted to trade.

Captain Sousa permitted only a few natives to board his ship, but he noticed many of them swarming aboard the flagship. Nervous about the situation, he sent Magellan over to the flagship in a skiff to warn Sequeira of the danger. Magellan found the commander in his cabin playing chess with a Malay nobleman. Eight other armed Malays also stood in the cabin, probably waiting for the signal to attack. Without alarming the Malays, Magellan informed Sequeira that the ship was surrounded by possibly hostile natives. At once, Sequeira cleared his cabin of visitors and ordered the natives off his ship. On shore, a mob had moved between the transport party and its boats. The trap had been sprung.

Seeing that they had been cut off, most of the men on shore fled toward the warehouse. But Serrão and some of the others tried to fight their way through the mob to the boats.

Meanwhile, Magellan and two other men jumped into the skiff and raced to the beach, where they recaptured one of Serrão's longboats and fought off the Malays long enough for Serrão and those with him to pile into the boat. They then fought their way through the sampans back to their ships. Many of the shore party who fled toward the warehouse were captured. The rest, who tried to fight their way back to the beach, were killed. In the end, more than half of the transport party were killed or captured.

The incident shattered Sequeira's hopes of establishing a post at Malacca. Most of the captains wanted to try to rescue their captured shipmates and bombard the city in retaliation. However, Sequeira took a more cautious approach. He offered the sultan a ransom in exchange for the captives. He waited for two days but received no response. Worried that the favorable monsoon winds would soon shift, he gave up on a rescue plan. He ordered the fleet to set sail for India, leaving the rest of the men behind.

Shortly after leaving Malacca, the vessels encountered a large, richly laden junk. In those days, Portuguese adventurers considered the Indian Ocean their own private lake, and they did not think of seizing foreign vessels as piracy. The junk was captured and bound to the flagship, and a crew of 28 men went aboard and locked the Malay crew below deck. Refusing to give up their ship, the Malays knocked a hole in the junk below the waterline. Immediately, the boat began to sink. Afraid the junk would sink and take the flagship down with it, Sequeira ordered the rope cut, leaving his men adrift in the foundering ship. Their cries faded into the distance as the current carried the sinking junk back toward Malacca. Magellan and another crewman—Castelo Branco—denounced Sequeira's decision, calling it a disgrace. "Never could there be a better prize," Magellan argued, "than to save the lives of our men on that junk!" Irritated but swayed, Sequeira ordered the two men to rescue the others. They took the longboat and several other shipmates and succeeded in saving the men.

Misfortune continued to plague Sequeira. One of his caravels was wrecked in a storm, and another vessel was so badly damaged that it was beached on a small island and dismantled. The remaining ships finally made landfall at Travancore, a region on the Malabar Coast south of Cochin. Sequeira then sailed for Portugal, while some of the others made their way back to Cochin, including Magellan and Serrão.

In January 1510, Magellan and Serrão arrived back in Cochin, where Alfonso de Albuquerque had taken over as viceroy of India. Toward the end of the month, Magellan left Cochin on a cargo vessel bound for Lisbon. However, his homeward journey was short-lived. The ship he boarded was one of three carrying spices and other goods that had been accumulated since Almeida left India in March 1509. One ship left on schedule, but the other two—on one of which Magellan was a passenger—were delayed. On the third night out, the ships ran aground on Padua Bank near Laccadive Islands. The passengers and crew of both ships climbed into the lifeboats and landed on a nearby islet. Although the ships were damaged, they were able to salvage most of the cargo of pepper and a good supply of fresh water and food. But no one knew they were stranded. The longboats would have to sail to the mainland, more than 100 miles (160 kilometers) to the mainland to get help.

Worried the officers would not return to rescue them, some of the passengers surrounded the longboats and would not let them shove off the beach. Understanding their concerns, Magellan said, "Let the captains and gentlemen go, and I will remain with you sailors if they will give us their word of honor that upon arriving [on the mainland] they will send help for us!" As the officers prepared to depart, Magellan was in one of the boats discussing the unloading of cargo. One of the sailors on shore spotted him there and called out, "Oh, Mr. Magellan

Sir, didn't you promise to stay with us?" Magellan assured the sailor he was staying. Leaping onto the beach, he shouted, "See me here!" The two longboats reached Cannanore eight days later. Immediately, the officers sent a caravel to rescue the shipwrecked men and the pepper.

In October 1510, Magellan tried to make a business deal that would secure him a nice profit when he finally returned to Lisbon. He signed a contract with Pedro Annes Abraldez, a merchant who was preparing to sail for home with the annual flotilla. According to the terms of the contract, Magellan would lend Abraldez 10 portugueses (gold coins each worth 10 silver cruzados, or $300) to purchase pepper. In return, Abraldez would pay Magellan back when they got to Lisbon, plus interest on his investment, as well as a portion of the sales. Because pepper could be sold at a high price in Portugal, Magellan stood to make an enormous profit off of the deal. The flotilla set sail in March 1511, but Magellan stayed behind, planning to go home with another flotilla.

For the next two years, Magellan served as one of Albuquerque's captains. Finally in 1513, after eight years in the Orient, Ferdinand Magellan arrived back in Lisbon. His happy homecoming was short-lived, however. He learned that Abraldez had died, and the merchant's father had fled to Galicia to escape his son's creditors. Magellan had invested his entire fortune with Abraldez, and now it looked as though he would never get any of it back. For Magellan, circumstances seemed like they could not get any worse. Soon, however, a shattering experience would force him to leave his native land forever.

A New Homeland

EARLY IN 1513, MULEY ZAYAM, GOVERNOR OF AZAMOR (Azemmour) on Morocco's Atlantic coast refused to pay an annual tribute owed to Portugal. Anticipating an attack, Zayam prepared an army to defend the city from Portuguese soldiers. Meanwhile, King Manuel was determined to put down the rebellion and discourage other Moroccan territories from imitating such acts of defiance. He quickly assembled an army of 500 ships, 13,000 foot soldiers, and 2,000 cavalry soldiers—the largest military force ever to sail from Portugal. Magellan and his brother Diogo had been called up to serve in a cavalry unit commanded by Captain Aires Telles. Each cavalry soldier brought his own horse, no small expense for Magellan, who was already struggling with finances. On August 13, 1513, the fleet set sail under the command of the king's nephew, the duke of Braganza.

During the battle at Azamor, one of the city's defenders speared Magellan's horse with a lance, killing it. Magellan barely escaped with his life. The city quickly surrendered after a cannonball struck and killed the Azamor general. However, the desert warriors outside the city put up a greater fight. Even after the city fell, they continued to launch raids against the Portuguese. After finding a replacement horse, Magellan bravely rode out each day to help defend the captured city. In one skirmish, an enemy lance stabbed him in the knee, leaving him permanently crippled. For the rest of his life, he walked with a limp.

As payment for the loss of his horse, the unit quartermaster offered to pay Magellan 3,700 reis. The usual rate paid to an officer whose horse had been killed in battle was 13,000 reis. Obviously, Magellan was enraged. Instead of going to his captain, he went over the heads of his superiors and wrote a letter to King Manuel. Manuel was not known for his generosity—even to those who had faithfully served him. In his view, Magellan's letter was a pesky nuisance. He was busy with more important affairs and did not want to be bothered by petty problems. The king chose to ignore Magellan's plea for justice.

Magellan was rewarded in another way, however. Because of his courage in battle, he was appointed quartermaster-major, a position of high rank. Many officers desired this post because it involved the job of distributing the spoils of war. The senior officers resented the promotion of a junior officer to such a prized post, and they looked for ways to get Magellan fired.

In March 1514, an army of Azamor natives launched an attack on the Portuguese. After a bloody fight, the Portuguese managed to drive back the enemy, thanks in part to some native tribesmen who helped the Portuguese in the battle. As the Azamor army fled, it abandoned a huge herd of livestock made up of about 200,000 goats and 3,000 camels and horses. Magellan and the other quartermaster-major, Captain Álvaro Monteiro, were put in charge of distributing the spoils fairly among the soldiers. Because they did not have proper corrals to confine and separate the animals, it proved impossible to make an accurate count. In an effort to whittle down the size of the herd, Magellan and Monteiro allowed the tribesmen who helped the Portuguese to take some of the goats. The jealous officers who resented Magellan saw this incident as an opportunity to discredit him. They accused him of selling to the enemy and keeping the money for himself. These charges were serious ones. Not only had they accused Magellan of stealing from the king, they had suggested that he had helped the enemy—or committed treason—a crime punished by death.

Knowing that the charges were ridiculous, Magellan did not take them seriously. He had given King Manuel years of loyal service. Surely, the king would not even consider the rumors to be true. He ignored the charges and even left his post without permission to travel to Lisbon to see the king personally. Expecting Magellan to offer a defense against the charges of corruption and treason, King Manuel agreed to see him. Rather than denying or even acknowledging the rumors, Magellan instead asked the king for an increase in his *moradia*, an allowance paid to members of the royal household. Annoyed by Magellan's arrogant behavior, King Manuel scolded him for leaving his post without authorization and reminded him that serious charges against him were still pending. He refused to grant Magellan's request and ordered him back to Morocco to face the charges. Outraged, Magellan obeyed the king's orders and returned to Azamor. An investigation revealed what Magellan already knew—the accusations were unfounded.

With the charges were dismissed, Magellan returned to Lisbon and again asked the king for a raise. He craved the recognition he believed he had earned through years of devotion and sacrifice. However, King Manuel seldom rewarded his faithful subjects. When Vasco da Gama had requested a bonus for his soldier and sailors after they had won a battle at Calicut, Manuel had staunchly refused. He had rewarded Almeida's naval victory at Diu by replacing him with Albuquerque. King Manuel was not about to reward Magellan either.

Frustrated but persistent, Magellan tried another avenue. He implored the king to allow him to take men, arms, and supplies to the Moluccas Islands, otherwise known as the Spice Islands, to help his cousin Serrão establish an outpost there. There were rumors that Portugal's rival—Spain—was planning to set up a trading post in this valuable territory. Magellan thought it would be wise for Portugal to build one first. Serrão, who had stayed in India, had made notable achievements in the Spice Islands and at the time was living richly on Ternate—an island in the Moluccas of eastern Indonesia, located off the west coast of the larger island of Halmahera. Magellan's meeting with the king was a disaster. Not only did Manuel refuse to increase his allowance, he told Magellan that Portugal had no further interest in his services. In other words, King Manuel banned Magellan from all expeditions or military service. He no longer had a job with the royal court.

Dishonored by his country, Magellan asked if he was free to offer his services to another country. The king icily responded that he could go wherever he pleased. As one final act of respect, Magellan tried to kiss the king's hand farewell. Manuel yanked his hand away and turned his back on Magellan. Limping away in utter disgrace, Magellan had no way of knowing that the king's rejection would turn into his greatest opportunity.

Renewed Ambition

Magellan was convinced that establishing a post in the Spice Islands was an excellent idea. Serrão was the first Portuguese, and most likely the first European, to reach the Moluccas. He was a military adviser to the sultan of Ternate and the son-in-law of the sultan of Tidore—a neighboring island. Serrão was in a superb position to secure alliances and trade agreements that would grant the Portuguese control over the export of spices. But King Manuel was selfish and shortsighted. There was no chance Serrão could win him over.

In 1515, Magellan was around 40 years old, at a time when 50 or 60 was a good long life. He had little to show for his 25 years of service to the royal court, eight of those years being in military service overseas. With no estate, wife, or children, and only a crippled knee to remind him of his failed career, he saw his life slipping away before he had experienced any major accomplishment.

Across the border in Spain, crafty Ferdinand II—king of Aragon and regent of Castile—was scheming to overtake Portugal in the spice trade. Geographers and mapmakers had begun to question the line of the Tordesillas Treaty signed in 1494, which divided the newly discovered lands outside Europe between Spain and Portugal. The line of demarcation was about halfway between the Cape Verde Islands (off the west coast of Africa), which already belonged to the Portuguese, and the islands discovered by Christopher Columbus on his first voyage, which he claimed for Spain. The lands to the east would belong to Portugal and the lands to the west to Spain. The Spice Islands were believed to lay close to the treaty line, but court geographers were unsure on which side. They worried the prized Spice Islands might lie within the Spanish hemisphere.

Magellan found this news exciting. He was also fascinated by reports that the land across the ocean to the west was not a part of eastern Asia. In 1513, Vasco Núñez de Balboa had discovered a sea on the south side of the Isthmus of Panama. Since then, geographers had been speculating

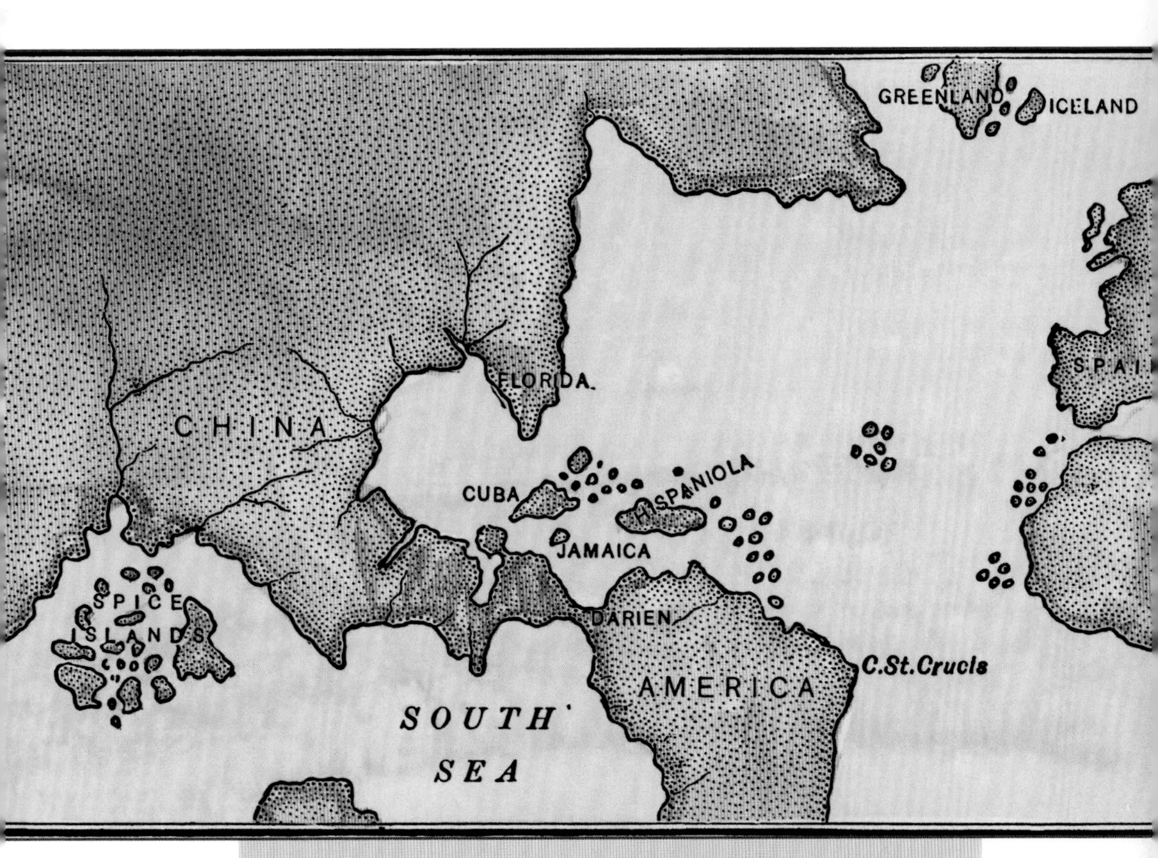

In 1493, after Columbus returned from his maiden voyage to the Americas, territorial disputes emerged between Spain and Portugal. Hoping for peace between the two powers, Pope Alexander VI drew a line on the globe, dividing the world in half. Portugal controlled the east side of the line, while any land found on the west side belonged to Spain. Like Columbus, Magellan thought that the Spice Islands (whose ownership was in dispute) could be reached by sailing west through the New World. This map of the New World made after the discoveries of Columbus and Balboa shows South America attached to Asia.

that there might be an edge to the landmass in the western Atlantic Ocean, one that could be sailed around. Or perhaps, there was a strait leading into Balboa's sea. Through mathematical calculations, most geographers came to the conclusion that it would be just a short haul across Balboa's sea to China and even a shorter one to Japan. With all these fresh speculations circulating, Magellan yearned for an opportunity to link up with Serrão and plan an expedition to the Spice Islands. The only trouble was that he had no country to back him up.

Magellan began spending long hours in the library and chartroom in Lisbon. He read over reports of earlier Portuguese explorers who had visited the coast of Brazil. He realized that the Spaniards were aware that the coast south of Brazil was on their side of the treaty line. Undoubtedly, they would intensify their exploration of the region. Magellan had first-hand information from his own experience in Malacca and from Serrão's letters to him. He believed this privileged information could be used to entice Spain into sponsoring his expedition to the Spice Islands.

Magellan's desire to lead a westward voyage was based on his belief that the Spice Islands did in fact lay in the Spanish hemisphere, east of the line of demarcation. He had to convince the Spanish court that he could reach the Spice Islands by sailing west and bring back to Spain proof of their location. If he could accomplish this, he might win their support. However, to establish the exact location of the Spice Islands, he would need an accurate method of determining longitude. It just so happened that Rodriguo (Ruy) Faleiro—famous mathematician, astronomer, and expert of the nautical sciences—held a grudge against King Manuel. Ruy and his brother Francisco agreed to pinpoint the location of the Spice Islands for Magellan. They used world maps from the highly esteemed Portuguese cartographers Pedro and Jorge Reinel. On their maps, made before 1519, the Spice Islands were clearly located in the Spanish hemisphere. After 1519, however, navigation manuals showed that the Portuguese domain extended about five degrees east of the Spice Islands, a figure very close to reality. Nevertheless, the Faleiros constructed a globe that supported Magellan's belief that Spain might have a legitimate right to those islands. In the fall of 1517, Magellan left Portugal brimming with high hopes and ambition. His new partner—Ruy Faleiro—would meet him in the Spanish region of Seville a few months later. In the meantime, both men swore to keep their plans secret until they could arrange a meeting with the Spanish king.

Royal Support

In order to gain royal sponsorship, Magellan needed someone respected from Spain who could speak on his behalf. He contacted Diogo Barbosa, an ex-Portuguese, like Magellan, who had switched his allegiance to Spain. Barbosa had become an influential resident of Seville, being made a knight in the Order of Santiago and a military commander. When Magellan arrived in Seville on October 20, 1517, he went straight to Barbosa's home, where he was warmly welcomed. In December, he married one of Barbosa's daughters—Beatriz. Barbosa provided his daughter with a dowry of 600,000 maravedis (about $84,000), a substantial amount for Magellan. Little is known about the relationship between Magellan and his new bride. They were together less than two years. During that time, Beatriz gave birth to a son, Rodrigo, and became pregnant with a second child.

In January 1516, King Ferdinand had died, and his grandson, Charles—the son of Joanna the Mad and Philip of Burgundy—took over the throne of Aragon. Charles was not only heir to Aragon, however. The Balearic Islands, Sardinia, Sicily, and the kingdom of Naples were also part of his inheritance from his father. Because of his mother's mental illness, he soon became ruler of Castile and León as well, as Ferdinand had done before him. For decades, Spain had been divided by differences. Suddenly, it was beginning to unite.

As Charles came to the throne, Spain saw the dawn of a new age. With Spanish holdings greater than those of France, and the still unmeasured vastness of the New World under his control, Charles must have realized he was destined to be a ruler of great importance. Charles was also the heir of Maximilian I, Holy Roman Emperor. Although it would be three years before he would inherit the lands under that monarchy—Germany, Austria, the Netherlands, and more. Born in 1500, Charles was only 17 when he took the throne. Because he was raised in Ghent, a city in Belgium, he spoke no Spanish. Yet, this youth was the person whom Magellan would have to convince of his grand idea. He had to place his hopes and future in the young hands of Charles I.

With some help from Barbosa, Magellan and Faleiro had their first meeting with Charles in February of 1518 at the royal court in Valladolid. As the spokesman, Magellan presented his arguments for the expedition clearly and rationally. Charles was immediately interested in Magellan's plan. He understood that if Magellan's expedition succeeded in locating the Spice Islands on the Spanish side of the demarcation line, the spice trade monopoly would be ripped away from Portugal and handed to Spain. Such an outcome promised huge profits for Spain.

On March 22, 1518, Magellan and Faleiro received an official commission from Charles. It had taken Columbus seven years to win grudging support for his expedition, but it took less than a month for Magellan to win enthusiastic approval. In Magellan's daring expedition, Charles saw an opportunity to beat the Portuguese to the Far East, make new discoveries, and build a worldwide empire. Shortly before Magellan and Faleiro left for Seville to make their arrangements, the king knighted them both and made them commanders of the Order of Santiago, the most ancient of all Spanish orders of

TRYING TO STOP MAGELLAN

In the 1500s, Portugal and Spain were entangled in a race to control the seas. At the time of Magellan's departure, Portugal held the lead. But if Spain were to find a westerly route to the treasured Spice Islands, the balance of power might shift to the Spanish. King Manuel did everything in his power to stop Magellan's expedition.

Just months earlier, Magellan had begged King Manuel to authorize an expedition. Now that Magellan had gone over to the enemy and gotten King Charles's approval, Manuel grew nervous. Manuel's ambassador in Spain wrote the Portuguese king a letter, as quoted in Tim Joyner's *Magellan*, describing Magellan as "a man of great spirit, very skilled in matters concerning the sea." But he believed Magellan could still be lured back to the Portuguese side. However, both Manuel and his council were opposed to inviting Magellan back to Portugal. Instead, they considered having Magellan murdered. Vasco da Gama, the Portuguese explorer who had discovered the route to India, openly criticized King Manuel for not having Magellan beheaded when he had the chance to do so.

In Spain, Ambassador Álvaro da Costa desperately tried to convince Magellan that his service to Spain was treason against his homeland. Unmoved, Magellan assured Costa that the Spanish fleet would not infringe on Portugal's legitimate land claims. Costa pressed King Charles and his counselors to cancel the expedition. But the young leader could not be swayed.

When it became obvious that the expedition would go ahead as scheduled, King Manuel decided he would try to stop Magellan on the open seas. He positioned Portuguese warships along Magellan's proposed route. Shrewdly, Magellan anticipated Manuel's ambush. The sailing course he announced was a cover-up for the real route. To make sure there was no way his true course could be discovered, he told no one. Magellan's secrecy led to problems within his crew, but he successfully dodged the Portuguese warships.

knighthood. Finally, after years without recognition in the land of his birth, Magellan found the support in Spain for which he had long been searching.

Back in Seville, Magellan threw himself wholeheartedly into the task of preparing the fleet for sea. Even the smallest details got his full and personal attention. He willingly pitched in, lending an extra hand to get the job done properly and on schedule. He secured rations of hard biscuits, salt beef, salt pork, cheese, dried codfish, and pickled anchovies. To this basic ship diet, he added ample supplies of dried beans and chickpeas, as well as onions, garlic, marmalade, honey, raisins, currants, olives, figs, almonds, and other nuts. While Magellan attended to outfitting the fleet, Faleiro managed scientific matters, such as supervising the preparation of charts, globes, and other navigational tables, as well as the gathering of compasses, astrolabes, and other navigational instruments. The five ships under Magellan's command were the *Trinidad* (Magellan's flagship), *San Antonio*, *Concepción*, *Victoria*, and *Santiago*. These ships became known as the Moluccan Fleet.

By early April 1519, the ships of the Moluccan Fleet had been reconditioned, armed, and outfitted with crewmen and supplies for the long sea voyage. Finally on August 10, under the thundering blasts of cannon, the ships of the Moluccan Fleet raised anchor, hoisted the sails, and pushed down the Guadalquivir River toward the port of San Lúcar. The fleet lingered there for more than a month while Magellan tied up all the loose ends and took care of any final business. He even signed a will, making sure his wife and children would be taken care of if he should not return.

At last, the morning of departure arrived. Just before dawn on September 20, the Moluccan Fleet weighed anchor. As the crew hoisted sails, the canvas snapped and billowed in

After 18 months of making repairs to his fleet, Magellan and his crew were able to tackle the task of stocking up his ships with supplies for the difficult journey ahead. Besides a huge store of food, the ships carried weaponry, including cannons, javelins, and crossbows, and items for trading such as fishhooks, small bells, combs, mirrors, knives, and bracelets.

the wind. Slowly, the five ships glided out of the harbor. They sailed toward the Atlantic Ocean to face a voyage of perils and hardships yet unknown.

To the Spice Islands

THE FLEET'S FIRST STOP WAS IN THE CANARY ISLANDS, A six-day voyage from San Lúcar. At the port of Monte Rojo, a courier rushed on board with an urgent message for Magellan from his father-in-law, Diogo Barbosa. Barbosa warned him of a possible plot to mutiny. Before the fleet had departed from Seville, several of the Castilian captains had openly boasted that they would oust Magellan from command at their earliest opportunity, even if it meant they had to kill him.

From the beginning, there were two opposing factions in the fleet. The Portuguese mariners and supernumeraries assigned to the *Trinidad* were sure to support Magellan. However, the Castilian high command on the *San Antonio*, *Concepción*, and *Victoria* were clearly aligned with Juan de Cartagena, the captain of the *San Antonio*. Then there were a number of crewmen who did not choose sides. They were simply focused on surviving the hazardous voyage and cared little about the politics of the fleet. For Magellan, the opposition

The government of Spain provided five ships for Magellan's voyage: the *Trinidad,* the *San Antonio*, the *Concepción*, the *Victoria*, and the *Santiago*. The caravels (broad-beamed ships with three masts sporting square sails and a triangular sail) covered about 100 miles per day. Above is a replica of one of Magellan's ships in San Julián, Argentina.

caused some concern. If the Castilian captains rose against him, Magellan could really count only on the members of the *Trinidad* to remain loyal to him. The crew of the little *Santiago*

FLEET OFFICERS

TRINIDAD		
Captain General	Ferdinand Magellan	Portuguese
Pilot	Estevão Gomes	Portuguese
Master	Juan Bautista de Poncevera	Genoese (from Genoa, a seaport in northern Italy)
Mate	Francisco Albo	Greek (from Greece)
SAN ANTONIO		
Captain	Juan de Cartagena	Castilian (from Castile, Spain)
Astrologer-pilot	Andrés de San Martín	Castilian
Pilot	Juan Rodríguez de Mafra	Castilian
Master	Juan de Elorriaga	Basque (from a region in north-central Spain and southwestern France)
Mate	Diego Hernández	Castilian

(Continues)

(Continued)

CONCEPCIÓN		
Captain	Gaspar de Quesada	Castilian
Pilot	João Lopes Carvalho	Portuguese
Master	Juan Sebastián del Cano	Basque
Mate	Juan de Acurio	Basque
VICTORIA		
Captain	Luis de Mendoza	Castilian
Pilot	Vasco Galego	Portuguese
Master	Antonio Salamón	Sicilian (from Sicily)
Mate	Miguel de Rodas	Greek
SANTIAGO		
Captain-Pilot	Juan Rodríguez Serrano	Castilian
Master	Baltasar Palla (Genovés)	Genoese
Mate	Bartolomé Prieur	French

could sway either way. Captain-Pilot Juan Rodríguez Serrano, although Castilian, was a deeply professional officer, likely to support the commander he found most competent to lead the fleet safely through the dangers ahead.

Nevertheless, Magellan sent a reassuring reply to Barbosa. He said that since the captains had been chosen by the king, he would do everything in his power to work with them in service of the emperor to whom they had all pledged their lives. In other words, he would not give them a reason to revolt. However, the crew soon found that Magellan was not always a pleasant and accommodating commander.

At midnight on October 3, the fleet weighed anchor and headed southwest. By midday the ships were nearing the Canary Islands. At this point, Magellan signaled a change of course to south by west. For the rest of the day, the *Trinidad* led the fleet, alternating between that course and due south. When the other ships approached the flagship for the evening salute, Magellan offered no explanation for the change in course. They continued in this route through the night and into the next day.

On October 5, the *San Antonio* pulled alongside the *Trinidad.* Captain Cartagena asked what course the fleet was running. Estevão Gomes, *Trinidad's* pilot, replied that the course was south by west. Then, an irritated Cartagena called out to Magellan, asking why the course they had all agreed on in Seville had been altered. He asserted that Magellan should not make such changes without consulting the captains, pilots, and masters of the other ships. He also argued that the southerly course they were running was a risky one. In a prickly response, Magellan told Cartagena that the other ships had to worry only about following his flag during the day and his farol at night. "You are to follow me and ask no questions," Magellan said, as quoted in Charles McKew Parr's *Ferdinand Magellan, Circumnavigator*.

Actually, the reason for the course change was a matter of safety. Knowing that King Manuel wanted to stop his expedition in any way he could, Magellan suspected that someone might leak their course to the enemy. Therefore, in Seville, he informed his captains of a route that would lead them southwest of the Canary Islands. In reality, he planned to follow a route sometimes used by Portuguese mariners heading for Brazil, following the African coast of Guinea south and then southwest to Cape São Roque in northeastern Brazil. However, he kept his true course a secret, so there would be no chance of the Portuguese finding out. Magellan's decision was a wise one. At that very moment, Portuguese warships were probably waiting for the fleet southwest of the Canaries. But they were waiting for a fleet that would never show up.

At the same time, Cartagena was right—Magellan's route held some risks. The fleet could be mired in the doldrums—the belt along the equator known for its calm winds—for weeks. If he sailed far enough south before crossing toward Brazil, he could perhaps avoid hitting this area of calm winds. Nevertheless, Magellan had no intention of revealing his plan to the Castilian captains.

The fleet held a southerly course for 15 days, passing between the coast of Africa and the Cape Verde Islands. Around Sierra Leone, the fleet encountered a series of tropical storms so furious the crews almost had to cut away the masts to keep from capsizing. When the storms subsided, the ships entered the doldrums. For sailing vessels that depended on the wind to carry them, this weather made for slow headway. The sails hung limp in the still, stuffy tropical air. In 20 days, the vessels logged only nine nautical miles. Because of the delay, Magellan cut back on rations, which led to grumbling among the hungry crewmen.

Cartagena and the Castilian high command were furious with Magellan for stubbornly withholding his reasons for leading them into the doldrums. They did not keep their resentment secret. One evening, the *San Antonio* hailed the *Trinidad* for the customary salute, but made a disrespectful change. Traditionally, the ship's mate would call out, "God save you, captain general sir, [ship's] master and good [ship's] company!" Instead, Cartagena had a regular sailor call out the salute, addressing Magellan merely as "captain" rather than "captain general." At Magellan's command, Gomes ordered *San Antonio's* master, Juan de Elorriaga, to give the salute in the proper manner. Cartagena shouted back that his best sailor had given the salute, but if Magellan preferred, he would have it spoken by a cabin boy. For the next three days, Cartagena refused to perform the evening salute at all.

Some days later, during an officers' meeting, Cartagena again brought up the question of their course. At first, Magellan just ignored him. Angered by Magellan's rude behavior, Cartagena became bitterly disrespectful. His ranting drifted beyond simple frustration to downright insubordination. At once, Magellan jumped up from his seat, grabbed Cartagena by the collar and yelled, "You are under arrest!" In a panic, Cartagena called to his fellow officers to seize Magellan—an open act of mutiny in front of witnesses. Not one of his countrymen made a move to help him. As punishment, Magellan had him taken to the main deck and bound in the stocks normally used on common sailors.

The other captains were appalled that a Castilian nobleman should suffer such incredible humiliation. They begged Magellan to release Cartegena into the custody of one of them. Anxious to put the matter behind him, Magellan agreed to hand the mutinous captain over to Luis de Mendoza, captain of the *Victoria*. He then chose the fleet accountant, Antonio de Coca, to replace Cartagena as captain of the *San Antonio*.

Finally, after rocking in the doldrums for three weeks, the sails rustled in a light breeze. The wind gradually increased in strength, and the ships began to move. Magellan ordered Gomes to take a southwesterly course, and the fleet headed across the Atlantic Ocean. On November 20, it crossed the equator. By November 29, the ships were off the coast of Brazil between Cape São Roque and Cape Santo Agostinho. They continued to hug the coast until they reached the harbor of Rio de Janeiro, on the morning of December 13.

By this time, the entire crew was tired, hungry, and on edge. Magellan was anxious to replenish his supply of firewood and fresh food and water. Rio de Janeiro was inhabited by friendly natives who were willing to share the abundant fruit, vegetables, fish, and meat with visitors. Therefore, it was a good place to drop anchor and let the men rest up. As soon as the ships appeared offshore, a group of natives paddled out in canoes to greet them. When the natives realized there were men onboard with glittering trinkets to trade, they swarmed on deck. "For a fishhook or a knife," one sailor wrote, "they offered five or six chickens; a pair of geese for a comb; for a small mirror or a pair of scissors, enough fish to feed ten people; for a bell or a ribbon, a basket of [sweet] potatoes that taste like nuts or turnips. For the king in a deck of playing cards such as we use in Italy, they gave me six chickens, thinking that they had got the better of me."

For almost two weeks, the men enjoyed relaxed duties and socializing with the natives. Eventually, the fleet had to be put back to sea. Magellan ordered work parties to clean, repair, and resupply the ships. By Christmas Eve, the fleet was ready to again set sail, and the men celebrated the Feast of the Nativity and Christmas onboard. On the morning of December 27, under full sail, the fleet headed west-southwest for Cape Santa María. At last on January 11, 1520, the fleet passed the cape, crossing the demarcation line. The land to the south and west could be legitimately claimed by Spain. This meant Magellan no longer had to be on the lookout for Portuguese ships. He could explore every inlet that might open a passage to the west. It was not, however, the Portuguese that were his closest threat at sea. It was the Castilians members of his own crew.

Disgruntled Revolt

The fleet proceeded cautiously westward, following the shoreline of the estuary of the Río de la Plata. The waters were so shallow the ships were in danger of grounding. As they moved along, Magellan decided that this area could not be the entrance to a strait as he had hoped but the mouth of a great river system. To be certain, he sent the *Santiago* upriver. For 15 days, the *Santiago* explored both the Paraná and Uruguay rivers, the major tributaries of the Río de la Plata.

Meanwhile, the rest of the fleet explored the south shore of the estuary. The crews spotted many natives, but Magellan would not let any of his men on shore. He recalled the tragic fate of Spanish navigator and explorer Juan Díaz de Solís who, four years earlier, had been killed and eaten in this area. While exploring the estuary, the fleet suffered two casualties. An Irish sailor aboard the *Concepción* fell overboard and drowned. Another sailor was fatally kicked in a brawl with another crewman and died. When the *Santiago* returned, the fleet headed south. The ships followed Brazil's coastline, passing by Cape San Antonio and Cape Corrientes—near the present-day beach resort of Mar del Plata—all the while searching for a westward passage.

After sighting Punta Delgada on Argentina's Valdez Peninsula, strong southwest winds forced the fleet to take anchorage in a small bay. Magellan sent six men in one of the ship's boats to an islet at the entrance of the bay to search for food and water. While they did not find any fresh water, they managed to kill a number of penguins and seals and loaded them into the boat. Just as they were about to shove off, a fierce storm arose, forcing them to spend the night on the island to face the bitter cold without proper clothing to keep them warm. When they did not return in the morning, their shipmates feared they had frozen to death or had been killed by the seals. As soon as the storm calmed, Magellan sent out a search party. The rescuers soon found the skiff pulled up on the rocky shore of the islet, but the men were nowhere in sight. Finally, they stumbled across the half-frozen sailors behind some rocks. They had survived the night by huddling near a steaming mass of seals.

Just as the sails were hoisted on the *Trinidad*, another storm arose. A violent gust struck the ship. It lurched sideways and the anchor cables suddenly snapped. The ship skidded toward the rocky shoreline. Magellan ordered the crew to drop the spare anchor. Luckily, it held, saving the ship from being smashed on the rocks. That night the tempest died down, but the next morning, an even more ferocious gale blew in, lasting three days. The winds blew so violently the forecastles of all five ships were ripped away, and the sterncastles sustained heavy damages. At last, the storm subsided, and the fleet sailed out of what the crewmen had been calling "that godforsaken bay."

The fleet continued nosing south, hoping to find a protected harbor where it could spend the winter. Eventually, it came to a narrow inlet that opened into a beautiful bay, the home of many penguins and seals. Magellan sent a shore party to search for fresh water. While the men were ashore, another terrible storm struck. It dragged on for six days, once again stranding the shore party. The men managed to survive the storm, living off of mussels tossed on the beach by the waves. However, they had been unable to find fresh water. The fleet would not be able to winter there.

Magellan continued to push south. The consistent southwesterly slope of the coastline led him to believe that this landmass, like Africa, would end in a cape. If he was unable to find a strait through the continent, perhaps he would still be able to sail around the cape into Balboa's sea. He was determined to use this route as a last resort, however. More pressing was the urgency to find fresh food and water. If he was unable to replenish his supplies, he would be forced to land the fleet near the Cape of Good Hope. If it was spotted by a Portuguese ship, King Manuel would be informed that Magellan's fleet had been seen along the Portuguese route to the Far East. This possibility would be a horrible embarrassment for both Magellan and King Charles.

Desperately, Magellan persisted in his search for a safe haven. Then, on March 31, 1520—the day before Easter—the fleet entered a bay that Magellan named San Julián, in honor of Saint Julian. Again, he sent a party ashore to scout for fresh water, firewood, and food. This time, the men found food and water. So, the fleet anchored for the winter.

Here, on the morning of April 1—Easter Sunday—the failed mutiny was launched. The voyage down the Patagonian coast of Argentina had battered the crewmen. They were weak, tired, and hungry, and when Magellan cut back their rations, there was much grumbling on the ships. Disgruntled sailors can become desperate, and the Castilian high command saw this moment as its chance to finally get rid of Magellan. That morning, Magellan summoned all hands but the deck watches ashore for religious services. Afterward, he invited the captains, pilots, and officers of the high command to dine with him on the *Trinidad*. Before returning to the *Concepción*, shipmaster Juan Sebastián del Cano went to find Juan de Elorriaga, master of the *San Antonio*, to inform him of the resolution the officers were preparing to give to Magellan. They had compiled a list of grievances as a formality, but they had already planned to overthrow the commander. Cano was unsure whether or not Elorriaga would join the mutiny. So, he left out the part about rising up against Magellan if the command refused to meet their demands. Neither Quesada nor Mendoza attended the service. As for the Easter banquet on the *Trinidad*, the only Castilian to show up was Álvaro de Mesquita, who happened to be a relative of Magellan's.

Just six days out of port, a plot emerged by three of Magellan's captains to murder the explorer. On April 2, 1520, Cartagena, Quesada, and Mendoza led an open revolt that was quickly put down by Magellan and those still loyal to him. Afterward, the crew was condemned to work in chains doing hard labor, and the leaders of the mutiny were executed.

After Magellan strategically extinguished the revolt (described in Chapter One), he imprisoned the rebel officers. Cartagena was taken to the *Trinidad*, where he was bound in shackles with his fellow mutineers, including Quesada, Cano, and his co-conspirators.

Immediately, Magellan ordered a court-martial. The lifeless body of Mendoza was even propped up to stand trial with the rest. However, his sentence had already been carried out. Forty of the mutineers were found guilty and sentenced to death. Mendoza's body was taken ashore, decapitated, and quartered. Quesada was also beheaded and quartered. The dismembered parts of the two captains were speared on a pole and set out as a warning against further rebellion. Although Cartagena was also found guilty of mutiny, Magellan did not sentence him to death. Instead, he once again imprisoned him in one of the ships. Because the fleet could not afford to lose so many men, the death sentences of the rest of those found guilty, including Cano, were reduced. Instead, with their feet in chains, they were put to work at the pumps, cleaning the filthy bilges, and other hard, disgusting labor.

In Search of the Strait

With the mutiny behind him and the gruesome display on shore reminding the rest of the crew not to cross him, Magellan put the men to work cleaning and repairing the ships. One of the first tasks was rummaging—unloading and organizing all of the ships' supplies. Some of the men built sheds on shore in which to store the provisions. Next, the reeking ballast was hauled out of the bilges to be washed clean of accumulated muck. Then, the ships were careened, and the crew replaced rotted planks, caulked leaky seams, and tarred the hulls below the waterline.

After the provisions had been lugged ashore, the men took inventory. They discovered that the suppliers in Seville had delivered only half of the two-year supply of rations. They had disguised their deceit by issuing two invoices for the same supplies. The remaining rations would last the crews only six months, not nearly enough for the rest of the trip. Worse, as it turned out, the land that surrounded San Julián lacked wild food and there was not much fresh water. What they could find was not very good. Magellan realized that if the crews spent the entire winter in San Julián, they would have to rely on ships' stores to survive. By spring, they would not have enough food for a long sea voyage. He decided they had no other choice than to resume the search for a westward passage as soon as possible.

The frigid temperatures brought misery to the entire fleet. Several men froze to death, and others suffered from frostbite. Once again, Cartagena saw his chance to exploit the men's agony and overthrow Magellan. This time, he enlisted the help of the French chaplain Bernard Calmette. Much to their disappointment, the crews had experienced their share of mutiny and were not interested in another rebellion. The plot was quickly exposed. Cartagena had exhausted Magellan's patience. This time, Magellan sentenced the two men to be marooned at San Julián when the ships set sail.

The *Santiago* was the first of the five ships to be reconditioned. Eager to find a strait leading west, Magellan dispatched the little ship to explore the coast to the south. On May 1, 1520, Serrano and his crew left the bay and slowly traveled south. On May 6, a lookout spotted an opening in the coast about 60 nautical miles (69 miles) from San Julián. Threading its way through the shoals, the *Santiago* sailed into a long, deep estuary, full of seals and penguins. Serrano named the place Santa Cruz, after the feast of the Holy Cross celebrated on that day.

At Santa Cruz, Serrano and his crew anchored in the harbor for nearly two weeks, hunting seals and smoking the meat. On May 22, they pulled out of the bay and continued down the coast. Suddenly, a violent storm struck, tearing away the *Santiago's* sails. A crushing wave hit the stern and carried away the rudder. The thrashing wind and waves drove the helpless vessel toward shore. Working frantically, Serrano rigged up a spare sail and used it to steer the ship into the beach. All but one of the 38-member crew were able to leap from the ship safely onto shore. Within minutes, the surf pounded the *Santiago* to splinters.

For eight days, the shipwrecked sailors were stranded on the beach. Finding no food, they decided to head to Santa Cruz by foot. After four days of struggling over the rough terrain, they at last made it to the estuary. There, the starving men feasted on fish. Serrano chose two strong young sailors to hike back to San Julián for help. After 11 days of trudging over the rugged coastline, the half-frozen sailors at last made it to San Julián. The weather was too stormy to risk sending another ship after the shipwrecked sailors, so Magellan sent a 20-man rescue party by land. Although it took more than a month, the fleet was finally reunited at San Julián.

From Serrano's reports, Magellan learned that Santa Cruz offered an exceptional winter anchorage—a much better one than San Julián. An abundance of fish, seals, and seabirds would make it possible for the men to gather plenty of food. Magellan decided that the ships should anchor there and gather up meat to smoke and to store for the upcoming voyage. He also hoped to salvage timbers or other useful items washed ashore from the wreck of the *Santiago*. On August 24, the remaining four ships of the fleet departed San Julián, watching the figures of Cartagena and Calmette, stranded on shore, grow ever smaller until they disappeared altogether. The fleet stayed at Santa Cruz until the men had sufficiently replenished the food supply. On October 18 (spring in the Southern Hemisphere), the remaining four ships weighed anchor and resumed the search for a strait leading west.

Westward Passage

On October 21, the lookouts spotted another opening in the coast. As the fleet neared the passage, the men saw that it extended a great distance inland. Magellan named the cape Cabo Vírgenes, because it was the day that commemorated the martyrdom of the Eleven Thousand Virgins of St. Ursula. The fleet turned southwest to investigate the bay. The ships passed a long, sandy point that protruded from the cape and named it Punta Vírgenes. Today this point is known as Punta Dungeness.

Magellan sent the *San Antonio* and *Concepción* ahead to explore the bay, giving the men five days for their reconnaissance. The two ships came to a passage leading west, a channel called the First Narrows. The channel emptied into a broad lagoon called Bahía San Felipe. Obviously, this channel would not lead them to the sea. With the *San Antonio* in the lead, the ships continued westward into the Second Narrows, another channel that opened into Broad Reach, a wide gulf stretching south. Because the water here was salty and deep and had a strong current, Mesquita and his pilot, Gomes, believed this channel would lead to the sea. They had found the strait for which Magellan had been searching. Mesquita turned back, eager to deliver the exciting news to his commander. The two ships sailed into Punta Dungeness, banners flying and guns booming.

The fleet retraced the route explored by the *San Antonio*, anchoring at Paso Real, a sheltered cove between Isla Isabel and the Brunswick Peninsula. That evening, Magellan called a meeting of his captains and pilots. He wanted their advice on exploring the broad waterway to the south. All but Gomes were in favor of pushing forward. Convinced that this strait was indeed a westward passage, Gomes wanted to return to Spain. He argued that they would run out of rations before they reached the Spice Islands. Magellan responded, ". . . Even though we may be forced to eat the leather chafing gear on the yards, we

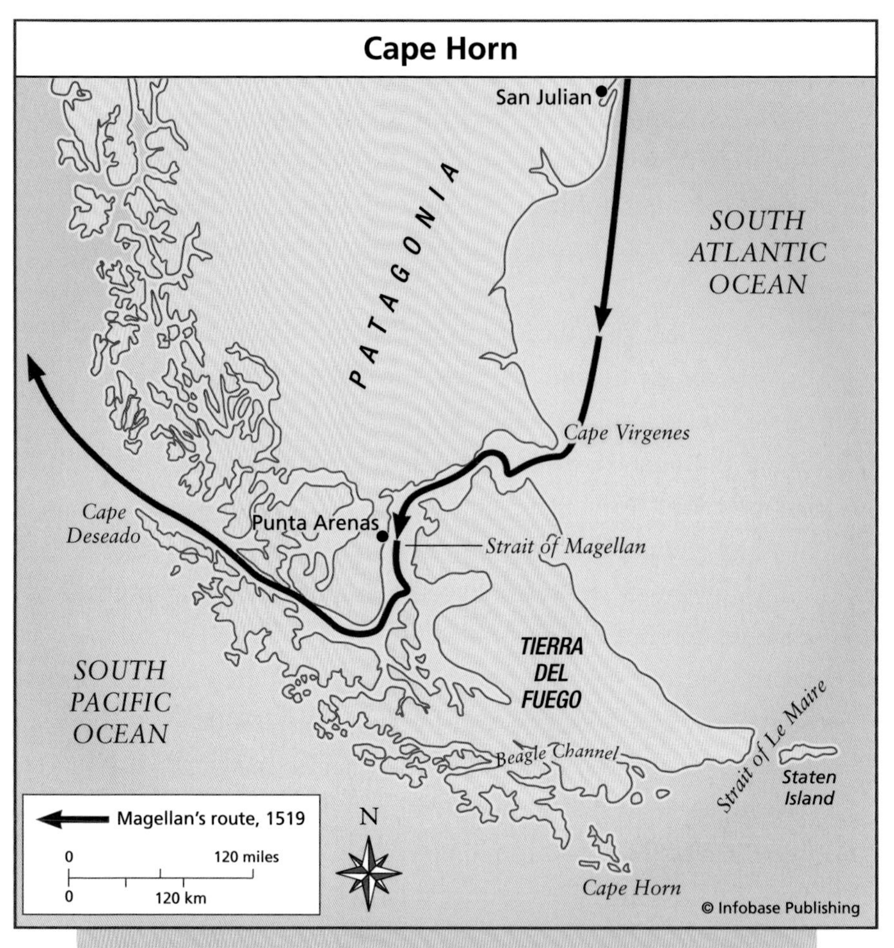

This map shows the route taken by Magellan around Cape Horn at the southern tip of South America. Magellan and his crew wintered at the bay of San Julián in December 1519. On October 21, 1520, the ships entered the passage later to be called the Strait of Magellan. They took over a month to travel through the strait, emerging into what Magellan named the Pacific Ocean.

must go forward and discover what had been promised to the Emperor."

Most of the high command knew that Gomes detested Magellan. After Cartagena had been arrested, Magellan

needed to choose a new captain for the *San Antonio*. Gomes believed he would be promoted from pilot to captain, but Magellan chose Mesquita instead. Bitterly disappointed, Gomes had held a grudge against his commander ever since. Outnumbered, Gomes would have to go along with the rest of the fleet.

The next day, the fleet headed south into Broad Reach. On the eastern shore, the men could see the native campfires burning at night. Magellan named the place Tierra del Fuego, the Land of Fire. Today this area is still known by this name. For many years, the name was fitting, even after the natives no longer burned campfires.

STRAIT OF MAGELLAN

The Strait of Magellan is 330 miles (530 kilometers) long and ranges from 2 and one half miles to 15 miles (4 to 24 kilometers) wide. Its waters extend westward from the Atlantic Ocean, between Cape Vírgenes and Cape Espíritu Santo. The strait curves northwest at Froward Cape until it opens into the Pacific Ocean. Discovered by Magellan in 1520, the strait separates South America from Tierra del Fuego and other islands south of the continent. Except for a few miles at its eastern end in Argentina, the strait mainly passes through Chile. Before the Panama Canal opened in 1914, the Strait of Magellan was an important passageway for sailing ships. It offered an inland route to the Pacific, far away from the almost continuous ocean storms of the region. One of the most scenic waterways in the world, Magellan's strait is still used by ships rounding South America.

By evening on November 1, the fleet came to a point where the strait divided into three water passages. Two led southward, and the other went east. This place is now known as Cape Valentín, which lies at the northern end of Dawson Island.

Magellan sent the *San Antonio* to explore the waterways leading east and south on the east side of the cape. After three days, Mesquita was to return to Cape Valentín and wait for the other ships. As Mesquita explored the channels east of Dawson Island, he came to Useless Bay, a blind passage. Next, he probed south into Canal Whiteside where he came upon another dead end.

Meanwhile, the other three ships sailed south into Famine Reach, the passage between Dawson Island and the mainland. Beyond Cape San Antonio, the channel breaks off into two branches. One branch, Froward Reach, stretches northwest. The other—Magdalena Sound—narrows to a channel leading south toward the snowcapped peaks of Mount Sarmiento. About 20 miles past the mountain, the channel curves west to the Great South Sea. Magellan could hardly contain his excitement. Too impatient to wait for Mesquita, he sent Serrano with the *Concepción* back to Cape Valentín. There, Serrano would meet up with the *San Antonio* and lead it into Froward Reach, where the *Trinidad* and *Victoria* would be anchored. But when Serrano reached Cape Valentín, there was no sign of the *San Antonio.*

Meanwhile, Mesquita had explored the channels to the east of Dawson Island, and then headed south into Famine Reach. He anchored the *San Antonio* in one of the small bays near Cape San Antonio. The landscape to the south was intimidating, with glacier-covered mountains spanning the horizon. Gomes used the icy surroundings to convince the other officers that Magellan was a madman who would lead them all to their frozen deaths. He proposed that they leave for Spain at once. However, Mesquita refused to abandon Magellan. A brawl broke out, during which Mesquita stabbed Gomes in the leg and Gomes jabbed Mesquita in the palm of his hand. The other officers jumped to Gomes's aid, grabbing Mesquita and binding him in chains. They tortured their captain into signing a statement that declared Magellan as a cruel commander, who had mistreated and murded the Castilian officers at San Julián for no reason.

Then, Gomes piloted the ship back through the strait, reaching the Atlantic Ocean on November 15, 1520. Worried about the dwindling food stores, Gomes headed straight for the Guinea Coast and Spain, without stopping at San Julián to rescue Cartagena and the priest, Calmette. The *San Antonio* arrived in Seville on May 6, 1521, with 55 crewmen onboard. Immediately, Mesquita, Estavão Gomes, and Gerónimo Guerra (who had taken over as captain of the *San Antonio* after Mesquita was bound) were arrested for abandoning the fleet. Gomes and his co-conspirators condemned Magellan, claiming that the expedition was a complete failure. They falsely stated that they were the last remaining ship, and all the others had perished on the voyage. Everyone but Mesquita was soon released. The authorities chose to believe Gomes and his henchmen rather than the loyal captain. Mesquita remained in prison until 1522, when the survivors of the fleet finally returned to back up his story.

Back in the strait, the *Trinidad* and *Victoria* rounded Cape Froward and headed into the part of the strait now known as English Reach. In search of a favorable spot to anchor, Magellan investigated a number of bays and coves. Magellan decided on Bahía Fortescue, 28 miles (45 km) west-northwest of Cape Froward. Although it was a day's sail from where Magellan had parted company with Serrano, and farther still from Cape Valentín, it offered the best anchorage to prepare the fleet for the ocean voyage ahead. Immediately after anchoring, the crews went to work making necessary repairs to the ships, cutting firewood, cleaning and filling the water barrels, and catching and smoking sardines.

In the Strait of Magellan, the crew enjoyed breathtaking views, like this one of the Chilean fjords. One of Magellan's crewmen on the *Trinidad*, Antonio Pigafetta, later wrote, "I believe that there is not a better strait in the world than that one."

By November 12, the *Concepción* had not yet returned with the *San Antonio*. Becoming worried, Magellan decided to weigh anchor and to go search for his missing ships. On the way, the searchers met up with the *Concepción*. Serrano reported that they had found no trace of the *San Antonio*. For the next six days, the remaining three ships embarked on a desperate search for Mesquita and his men. Being the largest ship in the fleet, the *San Antonio* carried a bulk of the provisions. Magellan was determined to do everything in his power to find it. He dispatched the *Victoria* toward the Atlantic entrance to the strait. Meanwhile, the *Trinidad* and *Concepción* would continue to search the area around Dawson Island.

The *Victoria* sailed all the way to Punta Dungeness but did not come across the *San Antonio*. On the shore there, Captain Barbosa erected a wooden cross and buried a message for Mesquita beside it. Magellan's men did the same on the west coast of Dawson Island. On November 18, the three ships assembled off Cape San Antonio. Neither search party had found the *San Antonio*. Magellan concluded that the ship must have sailed for Spain.

Undoubtedly, the loss of the *San Antonio* and its valuable provisions left Magellan dismayed. Still, he was determined to finish what he had started. The remaining three ships resumed their course up the strait. In light of *San Antonio*'s abandonment, Magellan decided to get more input from his crews. At their next anchorage, Magellan ordered that the captains, pilots, masters, and mates of his fleet submit, in writing, their honest opinions on whether the voyage should continue. Perhaps Magellan's officers were too afraid of his wrath to disagree with him. All of them expressed a desire to continue with the expedition.

On November 25, 1520, the fleet finally sailed out of what they called the Strait of All Saints (because Magellan's ships

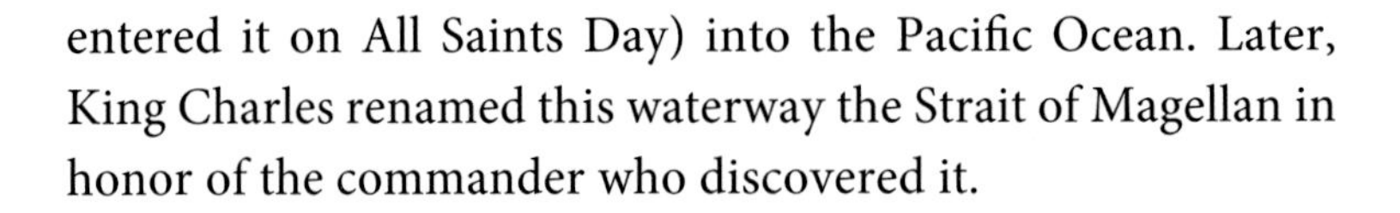

entered it on All Saints Day) into the Pacific Ocean. Later, King Charles renamed this waterway the Strait of Magellan in honor of the commander who discovered it.

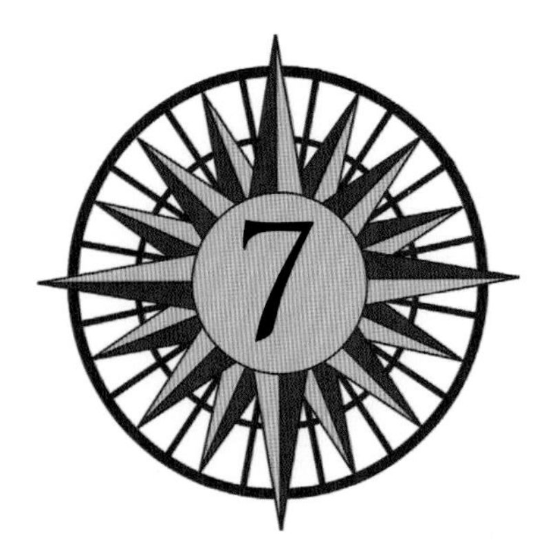

Sailing the Pacific

A GREAT, UNKNOWN OCEAN STRETCHED AS FAR WEST AS Magellan's eyes could see. The discovery of the Pacific Ocean has been credited to Vasco Núñez de Balboa, who got the first glimpse of it from a peak in Darien, Panama, in 1513. On November 15, 1520, Magellan became the first European explorer to sail its broad waves. When Magellan boldly sailed out of the strait, however, he had no idea of the vastness of the sea that spread before him. He knew only that somewhere on the equator—an undetermined distance away—lay the Spice Islands. He knew nothing about how far he would have to sail to get there or what might lie between. In fact, he had drastically underestimated the size of the Pacific Ocean in his original calculations. Because the waters of this ocean looked so calm and peaceful, Magellan named it *Mar Pacífico*, or peaceful sea. Little did he know this ocean was far from calm.

Magellan had great knowledge of the wind systems of the South Atlantic and Indian oceans. He had hoped these waters

At first, Magellan thought that the journey across the Pacific Ocean would be easy compared with the Atlantic. Instead, the men found that there was no place to stop for food and water. When the food was gone, the sailors ate rats, sawdust, and leather. Many starved to death or died from scurvy. It was several months before Magellan and his crew found an island with friendly natives willing to share fresh food.

would follow a similar pattern and was pleased to find out they did. Confident the voyage to the Spice Islands would be relatively short, he saw no need to risk landing on the mainland to replenish his provisions before embarking west. For the first part of the journey, luck played on his side. As noted in Tim Joyner's *Magellan*, "He could hardly have shaped a better course if he had had modern sailing directions, not only avoiding dangerous, island-studded waters, but making the best use of prevailing winds and currents."

The fleet continued northward along the Chilean coast, sailing between the mainland and the Juan Fernandez Islands. The crews failed to sight land, missing their last opportunity to replenish their food and water supply. By the end of December, the food left in the ships' stores had spoiled, and the water had gone rancid. The men began to fight over who got to eat the rats. "We ate biscuit that was no longer biscuit, but powder of biscuits swarming with worms," Pigafetta said in Tim Joyner's *Magellan*. "We drank yellow water that had been putrid for many days." Magellan's speech in the strait about eating the leather chafing gear proved to be an accurate prediction. "We also ate certain ox hides that covered the tops of the yards," Pigafetta continued. "We soaked them in the sea for four or five days, and then placed them briefly on hot ashes, and so ate them; often we ate sawdust."

Without fresh food, the men fell ill with scurvy. This deadly disease is caused by the lack of vitamin C, which is found in fruits and vegetables. Magellan's crew was deteriorating rapidly, and they were desperately in need of fresh food and water. Magellan steered the fleet in the direction he believed would bring it to landfall north of the Spice Islands. There, beyond the reach of the Portuguese, his men could recuperate before continuing. His target was probably Luzon, an island group in the Philippines. Faulty information had led him to believe it was Lequios, the Portuguese name for the Ryukyu Islands (a chain of Japanese islands in the Pacific Ocean).

Years earlier in Malacca, Magellan had heard about the wealthy merchants of Lequios. Before the Portuguese arrived in the Spice Islands, these merchants would travel to the Moluccas with gold from Luzon. They used the gold to buy junk loads of spices. Magellan probably confused Luzon, the source of the gold, with Lequois—the home of the merchants. Believing he was sailing to this gold island, Magellan

PEACEFUL SEA

The Pacific Ocean makes up almost one-third of Earth's surface, covering an area of 69.4 million square miles (179.7 million square kilometers). Its size is much larger than all of Earth's continents and landmasses combined. When Magellan first laid eyes on this magnificent sea, he called it *Mar Pacífico*, which means "peaceful sea" in Spanish. Although Magellan gave the Pacific a name, the ocean was first sighted by Spanish explorer Vasco Núñez de Balboa, who crossed the Isthmus of Panama in 1513.

The Pacific Ocean stretches approximately 9,600 miles (15,500 kilometers), from the Bering Sea in the Arctic to the icy fringes of Antarctica's Ross Sea in the south. Asia and Australia lie on the west side of the Pacific Ocean, and the Americas border it in the east. The Pacific Ocean opens its widest width between Indonesia and the coast of Colombia and Peru, where it stretches halfway around the world, about 12,300 miles (19,800 kilometers). About 25,000 islands, more than the total number in the rest of the world's oceans combined, dot the waters of the Pacific. Most of them are located south of the equator.

hoped to coax its rulers into forming an alliance with Spain. By the time his crews would have regained their health, it would have been late fall or early winter—the season of the northeast monsoon in the China Sea. With the wind at his back, Magellan could coast down to the Spice Islands to be reunited with his old friend, Francisco Serrão, who would be waiting for him.

On March 6, 1521, the lookouts spotted an island in the distance. As the fleet approached it, another island to the south became visible on the horizon. Today these islands are known as Rota and Guam (located between the Philippines and the Hawaiian Islands). As Magellan's ships sailed closer to investigate the area, a group of natives in long, swift sailboats came out to see them. The crewmen were impressed by the speed of these little outrigger canoes. The natives had cleverly rigged them with lateen sails—triangular sails mounted to an angled yardarm. The boats moved so quickly from wave to wave that one sailor said they looked like they were flying.

As soon as Magellan anchored off Guam, the curious natives climbed onboard. In their culture, visiting people were generous with each other. They went about the ship, scooping up any loose objects they liked. A few natives even made off with the *Trinidad's* longboat. Furious, the crewmen chased the natives from their ships. The natives believed they had done nothing wrong and that the Europeans had acted with rudeness. They returned later with an entire fleet of war canoes. To frighten them away, Magellan ordered blank shots fired from the *Trinidad's* deck guns. The thundering cannons startled the Guam natives, and they fled.

Still angry about the theft of his longboat, Magellan vowed to get it back and teach the thieves a lesson. The next day, he sent a well-armed party to shore. As soon as the men landed, some native warriors started hurling stones at them from a nearby ridge. Quickly, the crewmen fired their guns at the natives. Again, frightened by the strange-sounding weapons, the natives scattered. Moving inland, the shore party stormed a small village, burning the houses and boats and killing seven natives. After driving the natives out of the village, the shore party loaded the boats with coconuts and fruit and filled water casks in a nearby stream.

The punishment was enough to satisfy Magellan. On March 9, the ships left the island. After sailing west by south for a week, the crews could spot the mountains of Samar in the distance. The reefs along the coast of Samar prevented Magellan from attempting to land there. Instead, the fleet sailed south until it passed Sungi Point. The island of Suluan lay directly ahead, in the entrance to Lete Gulf. Near Suluan Island, the lookout spotted another small island (Homonhon, in the Philippines), about nine miles west. Magellan did not want to get into another scuffle with the natives. Because this island appeared to be uninhabited, Magellan decided they should anchor there.

The next day, Magellan had two tents set up on the beach for the men who suffered from scurvy. He went ashore daily to check on his sick crewmen. On March 18, nine natives came over from Suluan in a pirogue. The visitors seemed friendly, so Magellan invited them onto the flagship. Magellan offered them gifts of red cloth, combs, mirrors, bells, and ivory trinkets. Through hand signs, he indicated that he wanted to trade these items for fresh food. At once, the natives gave the commander all that they carried in their boat—a jug of palm wine, fish, two kinds of bananas, and two coconuts. Using gestures, they told Magellan they would return in four days with rice, coconuts, and many other kinds of food. Their word was good. On March 22, they arrived with lots of fresh food, including a chicken.

Many of the sick crewmen gradually recovered their strength, although during the past several months 19 men had died from scurvy and starvation. On March 25, the fleet set sail toward the coastline of Leyte in the Philippines. Then, turning south, the ships sailed through the Surigao Strait. On March 28, they dropped anchor in front of Limasawa, a small island off the southernmost tip of Leyte. At this place, an event proved that they had reached the eastern limit of the known world. A canoe carrying eight natives came out from Limasawa to inspect the ships. To Magellan's delight, his Malay slave, Enrique, understood the language. Magellan had acquired Enrique in Malacca in 1511. Apparently, Enrique had been raised in this area of what today is known as the central Philippines. He must have been sold into slavery, ending up in Malacca. Assuming this is true, Enrique was the first human to have completed a full trip around the world.

When he left on the expedition, Magellan had assured King Charles that the Spice Islands were located in the Spanish hemisphere, four degrees east of the treaty line. By this time, he had reached the eastern edge of southeast China, which he suspected included the Spice Islands. However, he found himself nine degrees west of the extended treaty line—in Portuguese territory. Nevertheless, unclaimed territory discovered and occupied by either country would be considered fair. Under this treaty provision, he could still establish trading posts and form alliances with local rulers before the Portuguese did.

Fatal Alliance

The eight curious natives who had canoed out to the fleet were too timid to get close. To show them that the Spaniards had come in peace, Magellan used a long stick to push a raft of gifts out to the canoes. The natives scooped up the gifts and took them back to the island. Two hours later, two barges approached the ships. A regal-looking native sat on one of them. His name was Colambu, ruler of Limasawa, Suluan, and Mindanao, the second largest island in the Philippines. When they pulled up to the flagship, Colambu sent some of his men onboard. Magellan gave them many gifts to take back to their chief.

The next day, Magellan sent Enrique ashore to negotiate with Colambu for fresh food. When Enrique returned, Colambu was with him. The chief boarded the flagship and offered Magellan two large fish and three porcelain jars filled with rice. In return, Magellan gave Colambu a hat and a red-and-yellow robe of fine Turkish cloth. He also gave Colambu's servants each a knife and a mirror. Then Magellan took Colambu on a tour of the ship. He ordered his gunners to fire some of the ship's artillery. The roar of the cannons awed and terrified his guests, but Magellan assured the chief that he had come in peace. Next, Magellan staged a mock battle to demonstrate the strength of a man in full armor. Colambu was impressed by the power of Spanish weaponry.

A couple of days later, Colambu's brother, Siaui, came out to the *Trinidad.* At once, Magellan ordered the ship's cook to prepare some food and invited Siaui and his three bodyguards to dine with him. Over the meal, Siaui—the ruler of several parts of Mindanao—told tales of the gold found in his territory. He said there was so much gold on an island near Mindanao that nuggets the size of hazelnuts and small fruit could be found in the beach sand. Undoubtedly, these stories excited Magellan, who became eager to form alliances with these wealthy chiefs.

The next day, March 31, 1521, would be Easter Sunday. Magellan decided to hold a religious service on shore. After a solemn Easter mass, Magellan presented the two chiefs, Colambu and Siaui, with a tall cross, adorned with a crown of thorns. He told them to place it on the highest point of the island, explaining that when Spanish ships saw this marker, they would know the islanders were friends. Magellan offered his ships and soldiers to help the chiefs defeat any of their enemies. Colambu and Siaui told Magellan that they were at war with two neighboring islands. As celebration for the alliance, Colambu and Siaui hosted a feast for the Spaniards.

Remnants of the original sixteenth-century cross erected by Magellan are contained in this hollow cross in Cebu City, in the Philippines. Scenes of Magellan erecting the cross are painted on the dome above.

During the celebration, Magellan learned that spices could be found at Leyte, Cebu, and Mindanao. Colambu promised to guide Magellan to Cebu, the main trading center of the region. On April 4, Colambu's barge led the fleet toward Cebu. Three days later, the barge and Magellan's ships nosed into the harbor and dropped anchor. Enrique and one of the sailors went ashore to deliver a message of peace to the local ruler, Rajah Humabon. Enrique explained that the Spaniards had come to purchase fresh food and to trade. Humabon replied that all trade ships must pay a tariff. Offended, Enrique told the chief that because his commander served such a powerful king, he would not pay tribute to any prince. He had come to the island in peace, but if war was what the ruler wanted, war he would have.

Intimidated by the thunder of the fleet's guns, Humabon decided to waive the port tax for his distinguished visitors. He even offered to pay tribute to their king and work out a trade agreement with the Spaniards. The following morning, Humabon sent his nephew to the *Trinidad* to secure a treaty of peace. After the treaty had been signed, the natives presented Magellan with several large baskets of rice and some live pigs, goats, and chickens. In return, Magellan offered the prince a bolt of fine white cloth and a cup made of gilded glass. He also sent gifts to Humabon, including a yellow-and-violet silken Turkish robe, a red hat, strings of glass beads, a silver dish, and two gilded glass drinking cups.

The next day, April 10, a party of crewmen set up a trading post in one of Humabon's merchant buildings. The store opened for business two days later. Of the products displayed, the natives liked the pieces of iron and bronze best, and they gladly traded their gold for some of these items.

One of the missions of Spanish expeditions was to convert natives to Christianity. On Sunday, April 14, Magellan held a religious ceremony and baptized 800 men, women, and children, including Colambu and Humabon and his family. Perhaps part of Magellan's missionary success was due to a faith healing he performed on a sick native. One of Humabon's relatives was too weak to go to the baptismal ceremony. Going to the man's house, Magellan found him so ill he could not even speak or move. Next to the dying man, his wife and daughters were making customary offerings to their idols. Magellan told the women if they would burn their idols and agree to be baptized, the power of Jesus Christ would cure the man. After the entire household had been baptized, Magellan asked the sick man how he felt. Miraculously, the man replied that he felt just fine. Then, Magellan gave him some almond milk to drink and ordered some of his crewmen to bring a mattress, sheets, blankets, and a pillow to the house. Each day, the patient drank a concoction of almond milk, oil, and water of roses, as well as some of Magellan's quince preserves. In less than five days, the man was walking again.

On the day of the baptisms, Humabon told Magellan that several local chiefs would not submit to his authority. Determined to crown Humabon the sole ruler of these islands, Magellan sent messages to the rebellious chiefs, ordering them to acknowledge Humabon as ruler. If they refused, Magellan warned, they would suffer death and destruction in their villages. Several of the chiefs still refused to bow to Humabon's authority. Magellan sent a small fighting force in two boats to punish one of the defiant chiefs. The soldiers burned his village—a town named Bulaya—and brought back much of its livestock.

Magellan then ordered the other stubborn chiefs to give Humabon a tribute of a goat, a pig, a basket of rice, and a jug of honey. If they failed to do this, Magellan promised to punish their villages the same way he had Bulaya. Two of the chiefs delivered the tribute, but Lapulapu, the Mactan island chief, still refused. Instead, he sent a message to the Spaniards. If they came to burn his village, he would be ready and waiting for them.

Enraged, Magellan declared that they would attack Lapulapu's village. His success at Bulaya made him feel invincible. He boasted to Humabon that he would need only 60 men to defeat the Mactans. He would personally lead the assault. Both Humabon and Serrano opposed the idea, but Magellan had made up his mind. At midnight on April 27, Magellan and 60 well-armed soldiers set out for Mactan Island. Their shallops were armed with portable swivel guns. In addition to swords and lances, the soldiers carried guns and crossbows. They were dressed in armor, but they chose to discard the leg armor so that they could easily climb in and out of the boats.

Lapulapu's village was at the northeastern end of the island. It was protcted by a fringe of groves. Humabon had warned Magellan to wait until daylight, because he knew the village would be surrounded by trenches with sharp bamboo stakes set in them. Nighttime attackers would fall into the trenches and be impaled by the spears. Instead, Humabon urged Magellan to let him lead the first attack, because he was familiar with the area. Magellan refused to listen, however. He insisted on his plan to wade ashore under the cover of darkness. Still, Humabon offered a force of 1,000 warriors in 30 war canoes to back up the Spanish army.

Just before dawn, Magellan and the men slipped into the shallow water, leaving boat crews to operate the swivel guns. Making it safely onto the beach, Magellan and his men headed straight for town. When they got to the village, they found it had been evacuated. Magellan ordered his men to start burning the houses. Suddenly, the natives surrounded and attacked Magellan's small force. For several hours, the Spaniards were able to fight off the defenders with their powerful weapons. Eventually, though, they ran out of gunpowder, lead, and crossbow arrows. The natives closed in, hurling stones, thrusting stakes and bamboo lances, and shooting poisoned arrows.

Realizing the fight had turned against them, Magellan ordered a gradual retreat. In a panic, most of the soldiers turned and fled, leaving their commander with only a few defenders to cover the retreat. Because the battle was too far inland, the natives were out of the range of the swivel guns. Magellan was trapped. Lapulapu's forces attacked with fury. Unwilling to give up, Magellan continued to fight the natives, even though most of his men had left him. Surrounded by the enemy, he was hammered with stones. One warrior slashed his leg, and

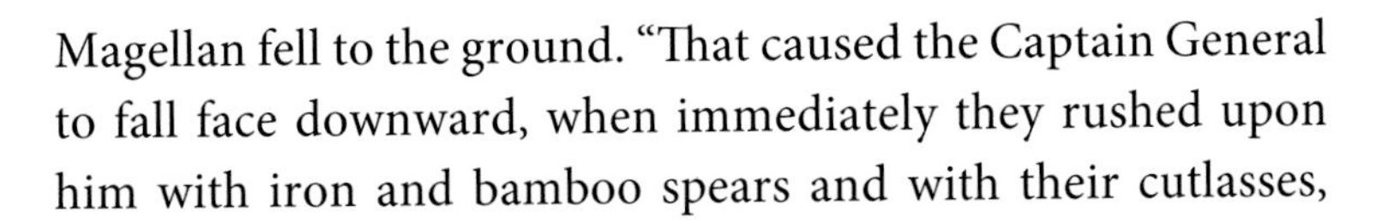

Magellan fell to the ground. "That caused the Captain General to fall face downward, when immediately they rushed upon him with iron and bamboo spears and with their cutlasses,

When Magellan tried to show force against the Mactan, he did not take into account that his ships would be anchored too far to help him and his crew. The Mactan rushed into the water, shooting arrows at the crews' legs. Magellan was killed short of successfully circumnavigating the globe.

until they killed our mirror, our light, our comfort, and our true guide," Pigafetta, who fought beside Magellan, later recalled, as quoted in Laurence Bergreen's *Over the Edge of the World*. "Beholding him dead," he continued, "we, wounded, retreated as best we could to the boats, which were already pulling off."

For some reason, Humabon did not land a single warrior to help the Spaniards. Apparently, Magellan had made a fatal alliance. At the moment of his death, the Cebuan warriors finally offered their aid. They charged into the water, holding their swords high in the air, and drove off the Mactan warriors. The Mactan did not show an urge to fight the Cebuan warriors. Perhaps Humabon and Lapulapu had worked together to trick Magellan and defeat the Spaniards. Meanwhile, the remaining soldiers scrambled into the boats and fled Cebu.

The death of Magellan shook Humabon's confidence in new allies and the power of their religion. On May 1, he invited the captains and officers to a ceremonial banquet. Barbosa was eager to go, but Serrano advised him to be cautious. They had just lost an important battle with Humabon's enemies. Serrano thought the banquet could be a trap to punish them. Barbosa mocked Serrano for being a coward. His pride stung, Serrano ordered the crew to prepare a longboat. He was the first to board it, followed by Barbosa. Affonso de Goes, the *Victoria*'s new captain also went along, as well as the ship's pilots, San Martín and Carvalho. A few other crewmen tagged along, including Espinosa, the priest, and Enrique.

When members of the shore party landed on the beach, Humabon warmly welcomed them. On the way to the banquet site, Espinosa and Carvalho noticed the prince (who had been miraculously cured by Magellan) quietly take the priest aside and escort the Spaniard to his house. Suspecting a trap, Espinosa and Carvalho hurried back to the longboat and rowed out to the *Trinidad*. Just as they were telling the rest of the crew about their suspicions, they heard shouting on shore. Their shipmates had been ambushed.

Carvalho ordered the ships to move closer to shore and bombard the town. As the gunners opened fire, one of the natives dragged Serrano—bound and bleeding—toward the beach. If the others had dared to risk rescuing him, it would have put the ships and their crews in jeopardy. Knowing this, Serrano shouted that it would be better for him to die than all of them. Following Serrano's heroic advice, the boats pulled away from Cebu, leaving him behind.

Around the World

When the fleet fled Cebu, all the original captains were gone, as well as most of its high command. Of the original pilots, just one remained—João Lopes Carvalho. As the senior officer, Carvalho took command. The survivors realized that there were not enough men left to operate three ships. Because the *Concepción* was in the worst condition, they decided to scuttle it. After dividing its crew, usable gear, and cargo between the other two ships, the men set fire to the *Concepción*. Carvalho was elected captain of the *Trinidad*, and Espinosa took over command of the *Victoria*. By May 4, 1521, all that remained of Magellan's once proud fleet were two ships. They set sail on a southwesterly course, along the islands of Panglao, east of Cebu.

By this time, the food supplies on the two ships were nearly exhausted. The crews had eaten most of the rice they had taken in Limasawa, and they were eager to replenish their supply. They sailed into the Sulu Sea, dropping anchor off of Cagayan Sulu Island, on the outskirts of the Philippines. The natives here were friendly and offered to supply the ships with all the food they needed. When the islanders delivered the food, the crews were dismayed to find that it was all perishable items—such as fruits and vegetables that would spoil quickly. The foods would sustain them for only a short time. However, they also learned from the natives that food could be obtained at Palawan, a large, lush island to the northwest. They set sail at once. Once they reached Palawan, they stayed there until they had completely restocked their ships' food supplies.

At the end of May, the ships left Palawan and continued on their quest to find the Spice Islands. On July 8, 1521, the two-ship fleet sailed into Brunei Bay and anchored there at the port. A fleet of pirogues came out to greet them. Brunei, in southeast Asia, was a large, bustling port city. The buildings along the waterfront were built up on pilings, and the harbor was packed with water traffic. Junks were anchored in the harbor, waiting their turn to load or unload cargo at the docks. It was obvious to the Spaniards that this was a highly civilized kingdom. Carvalho sent two native prisoners (who had been captured near Brunei) ashore to announce their arrival.

Six days later, three lavishly decorated boats carrying musicians circled the Spanish ships. The musicians serenaded their visitors with gongs and drums. Then the emissaries onboard offered elaborate gifts to the Spaniards. The sultan of Brunei had heard terrifying stories about the brutality of the Portuguese. Afraid that these strange visitors were scouts for a Portuguese fleet, the sultan was anxious to know more about their country and the reason for their visit. Carvalho and Espinosa assured the emissaries that the ships were not Portuguese but Spanish, and they were representatives of an emperor who desired only peace. Espinosa, Pigafetta, and five others were chosen to visit the sultan as a Spanish delegation on behalf of King Charles. Carvalho, being Portuguese, wisely stayed behind.

At the city docks, the delegation was met by an escort with two huge elephants. The Spaniards had never traveled in such grand style. When they reached the governor's house, they were treated to a sumptuous dinner. That night, they slept on cotton mattresses lined with taffeta and covered with sheets of fine cloth—a luxurious change from the putrid ships' cabins. At noon the next day, the delegation rode to the sultan's palace on elephants. The palace was surrounded with stone towers and heavily guarded with cannons. Like most of the buildings in Brunei, the place was set on stiltlike pilings, and the men had to climb a ladder to get to the entrance. They were led into a large hall crowded with Malay noblemen and women, wearing dazzling jewels and pearls and draped with silk sarongs embroidered in gold cloth. At one end of the main hall there were stairs leading to a small room. Inside, the sultan—Siripada—was seated with one of his young sons. One of the noblemen told the Spaniards that they must not speak directly with the sultan. If they wished anything, they should send one of the sultan's officials to speak for them.

The members of the delegation watched intently as each one of their gifts was presented to the sultan. They had brought a green velvet robe, a violet velvet chair, five yards of red cloth, a cap, a gilded drinking glass, a covered vase, three writing tablets, and a gilded writing case. For the queen, they offered three yards of yellow cloth, a pair of silvered shoes, and a silver needlecase full of needles. Although the Spaniards thought these were expensive gifts, they were not very impressive to a sultan of such exceeding wealth. As each one was displayed before him, he acknowledged it with only a slight nod. After all the gifts had been offered, the curtains in the doorway were closed, and the Spaniards could leave.

For about three weeks, the Spaniards freely roamed about Brunei, exchanging trade goods for much-needed provisions. Relations soon turned sour, however. For some reason, three armed junks suddenly anchored near the Spanish ships, blocking their exits out of the harbor. Carvalho suspected this action was part of another plot to trap them and placed his crews on alert. His suspicions were further aroused when three crewmen, who had been sent ashore, failed to return. On the morning of July 29, a fleet of more than 200 pirogues left the port of Brunei and headed straight for the fleet. Afraid of being trapped, Carvalho ordered the ships to weigh anchor. Then, he ordered the crew to open fire on the junks blocking their escape from the harbor. The ships sailed out of the harbor, intending to stop at a nearby island.

The next day, the fleet returned to the bay and captured the crew of one of the junks. One of the men captured was a young prince, the son of a rajah on Luzon. Carvalho hoped to use the prisoners as ransom for his own men. Foolishly, however, Carvalho made a private deal with the Luzon prince, releasing him in return for a large amount of gold, which the commander kept for himself. In return, the prince promised to get Carvalho's men released. Four days passed, and the sultan still refused to free the Spanish sailors. Finally, Carvalho gave up and set sail without his men.

After leaving Brunei Bay, the two ships sailed northeast along the coast of Borneo. Without an experienced pilot, it proved to be a dangerous task. The area turned out to be a maze of treacherous islets and reefs. They managed to find a safe anchorage near a small island off the north coast of Borneo. The island provided a beach suitable for careening, and the ships were in need of repair. The fleet anchored on August 15, and all hands pitched in to repair the worm-ridden hulls of the two ships. On September 21, the crews voted to oust Carvalho as their captain general. They were disgusted with his incompetent piloting and poor leadership. They chose Espinosa to take his place.

With the repairs completed, the fleet set sail on September 27, again in search of the coveted Spice Islands. Behaving like pirates, the Spaniards treated any native vessel as fair game. When they spotted a large junk, they captured and looted it. This behavior was not uncommon, however. In these seas, piracy was a way of life. Moreover, their commander, their captains, and most of their pilots were dead. The fleet was vulnerable and lost. They had only their superior weapons to depend on, and they could use their power to capture junks that might very well have done the same to them.

Heading south through the Celebes Sea to Sangi Island, the *Trinidad* and the *Victoria* then headed east, finally passing into the Molucca Sea—where the Spice Islands were located. Off in the distance, the crew spotted the tall peak of Ternate. The ultimate goal of Magellan's grand expedition lay directly ahead of them. The next peak to appear on the horizon was on Tidore, an island just south of Ternate. Nearly 27 months had passed since Magellan's fleet had set sail from San Lúcar. Of the five original ships, only two remained. Out of 270 men, just 107 had survived to see the Spice Islands.

On Friday, November 8, 1521, the *Trinidad* and *Victoria* sailed into the harbor of Tidore. The location of the Spice Islands turned out west of the line of demarcation and clearly within the Portuguese hemisphere. However, this knowledge did not deter them from seeking friendly terms and alliances with the rajah of Tidore and his allies. When they arrived, crewmen had expected to be greeted by Serrão, Magellan's long-time friend who had been serving as a military adviser to the rajah of Ternate. On asking about him, they learned that he was dead. In a plan to promote peace, Serrão had forced the rajah of Tidore—Almanzor—to give his daughter in marriage to the rajah of Ternate. In bitter resentment, Almanzor had poisoned Serrão.

Both the rajah of Tidore and the princes of Ternate were fed up with the Portuguese. They were willing to enter into an alliance with Spain. The Spaniards were allowed to load mace, a spice made from the inner layer surrounding nutmeg (the seed of a tree fruit), as well as sandalwood and bales of cloves. With their holds crammed full of spices and exotic goods, the two ships were ready to sail on December 18. The *Victoria* left first and waited outside the harbor for the other ship. The *Trinidad's* anchor snagged on the sea floor. As the crew struggled to free it, the anchor line pulled open a seam below the waterline of the boat. All at once, water gushed into the bilge. The *Trinidad* had to remain at Tidore until the necessary repairs could be made. The *Victoria* sailed on, taking advantage of the season's southeast winds to sail home.

It took nearly four months to repair the *Trinidad's* hull. Espinosa, who stayed with the flagship, made a bold decision to cross the Pacific from west to east. He reasoned that if they sailed far enough north, they would encounter westerly winds like those of the North Atlantic, and these winds would carry them to the eastern shore. Unfortunately, they knew nothing of the wind patterns in the Philippine Sea. Between January and June, the monsoon over Central Asia blows from the northeast. The westerly monsoon of the Spice Islands, which began soon after the *Victoria* departed, would carry the *Trinidad* only as far as the Philippine Sea. At that point, it would run head on into the monsoon.

Finally, on April 6, 1522, the *Trinidad* set sail, carrying 54 men and about 50 tons of cloves. The ship's first stop was on the west coast of Gilolo. From there, the *Trinidad* headed east by north. The light westerly winds soon yielded to the northeast monsoon, and the headwinds gradually became stronger. Realizing they had misjudged their route, the pilots ordered a change of course and steered the ship north. After the ship had battled the northeast headwinds for a month, the lookout spotted one of the northern Mariana Islands on June 11. When they anchored there, many islanders came out to greet them. One of the natives agreed to accompany them as a pilot.

Of the five ships that Magellan and his crew started with, the *Victoria* was the only one to complete the voyage. Of the 270 crew members, only 18 returned alive.

As the *Trinidad* climbed into ever higher latitudes in search of westerly winds, the temperature dropped. Lacking proper clothing, the crewmen suffered from the cold. They also started showing signs of scurvy. Even though the men saw seals and tuna, they were too weak from hunger, disease, and cold to try to catch them. In July, Espinosa decided the only way to survive would be to return to Gilolo. The return voyage took a heavy toll on the crew. After two weeks, survivors were pitching at least one dead body overboard each day. Of the 52 crew members, 33 had died by the time they reached Gilolo six weeks later.

With only seven men healthy enough to work the ship, Espinosa knew he needed help. At Gilolo, he received news that just 15 days after their departure from Tidore, a Portuguese fleet of seven ships had sailed into Ternate. Espinosa realized he had no other choice than to ask the Portuguese for help. He sent the ship's clerk—Bartolome Sanchez—to Ternate. Sanchez carried a letter to the Portuguese commander, Antonio de Brito, pleading for him to send a caravel with provisions to help the *Trinidad.* When Sanchez arrived in Ternate, Brito threw him in prison and refused to send help to his shipmates.

Brito waited until he knew the Spaniards would be too weak to fight. Then, he stormed the *Trinidad*, taking control of the ship and stealing its books, papers, charts, navigational equipment, and guns. The Portuguese even took the crew's personal belongings. They moved the *Trinidad* to Ternate and imprisoned its surviving crewmen.

Lone Ship Returns

On September 6, 1522, the *Victoria* and its 21 exhausted survivors (18 Spaniards and 3 Spice Islanders) sailed into the harbor at San Lúcar. In just under three years, the battered little ship had completed the first circumnavigation of the world. One witness described the scene: "On that ship, with more holes in it than a sieve, [were] 18 [Europeans], skinnier than an underfed old nag."

After the crewmen of the *Victoria* gave their accounts of the voyage, and what happened at San Julián, court officials finally released Álvaro de Mesquita from prison. Brought back to Spain in chains after Gomes had taken over his ship in the Strait of Magellan, he had suffered in prison ever since the return of the *San Antonio* in March 1521.

Because of the charges brought against Magellan by Gerónimo Guerra and Estevão Gomes, Magellan's wife, Beatriz, was placed under house arrest to keep her from fleeing to Portugal. The child she had been pregnant with when Magellan set sail was stillborn in 1520. Their infant son, Rodrigo, died in September 1521. Beatriz probably learned that her

An 1891 print shows a parade in honor of Magellan in Spain in 1522. The return was achieved under the command of one of Magellan's captains, Juan Sebastian Elcano.

husband had died before the *Victoria* returned to Spain. She died in March 1522, six months before the *Victoria* returned to San Lúcar.

Of the 54 men who sailed from Tidore with the *Trinidad* on April 6, 1522, only 4 lived to return to Spain: Gonzalo Gómez de Espinosa, León Pancaldo, Ginés de Mafra, and Juan Rodríguez. Of the entire crew of 260 to 270 men who set sail from San Lúcar with Magellan in 1519, 35 eventually returned to Spain. The *Victoria*, the only ship of Magellan's fleet to complete the first voyage to circumnavigate the globe, made two more voyages. It sank on the last voyage, taking all onboard into the sea with it.

Like most of his shipmates, Magellan forfeited his life for the expedition. For his family, the endeavor brought grief and ruin. The expedition's main objective—to bring back proof that the Spice Islands were on the Spanish side of the line of demarcation—was a failure. The small profit gained from the sale of the *Victoria's* cargo could never make up for the expense of the voyage. Still, Magellan's voyage represents a triumph of the human spirit. The circumnavigation also brought invaluable knowledge of the true size of the world and the span of its oceans. In history, Magellan's achievement stands unparalleled. For centuries to come, his feat will continue to inspire others to push their boundaries to the ultimate limit.

Chronology

c.1470–1480	Ferdinand Magellan born to Rodrigo de Magalhães and Alda de Mesquita.
1488	Portuguese explorer Bartholomew Diaz rounds the Cape of Good Hope.
1492	Genoese explorer Christopher Columbus sails west and reaches the Bahamas (funded by Spain); Magellan and his brother Diogo serve as pages in the Portuguese royal court.

TIMELINE

1470–1480
Ferdinand Magellan born to Rodrigo de Magalhães and Alda de Mesquita

1505
Magellan and his brother join the expedition of Portuguese explorer Francisco de Almeida to India; Magellan remains in service in the Indian Ocean until 1511

1513
Magellan is wounded, then falsely accused of treason; the charges are later dismissed

1514
Requests permission to sail to the Spice Islands; renounces Portuguese nationality when request is denied

1493	Pope Alexander VI divides the world into two spheres, one Spanish and one Portuguese.
1505	Magellan and his brother join the expedition of Portuguese explorer Francisco de Almeida to India.
1505–1511	Magellan is in service in the Indian Ocean.
1511	Francisco Serrao reaches the Spice Islands.
1513–1514	Magellan takes part in the Portuguese expedition to Morocco and is wounded; is falsely accused of treason; the charges are later dismissed.
1514	Requests permission of King Manuel of Portugal to sail to the Spice Islands in the Far East; the request is denied; Magellan renounces his Portuguese nationality.

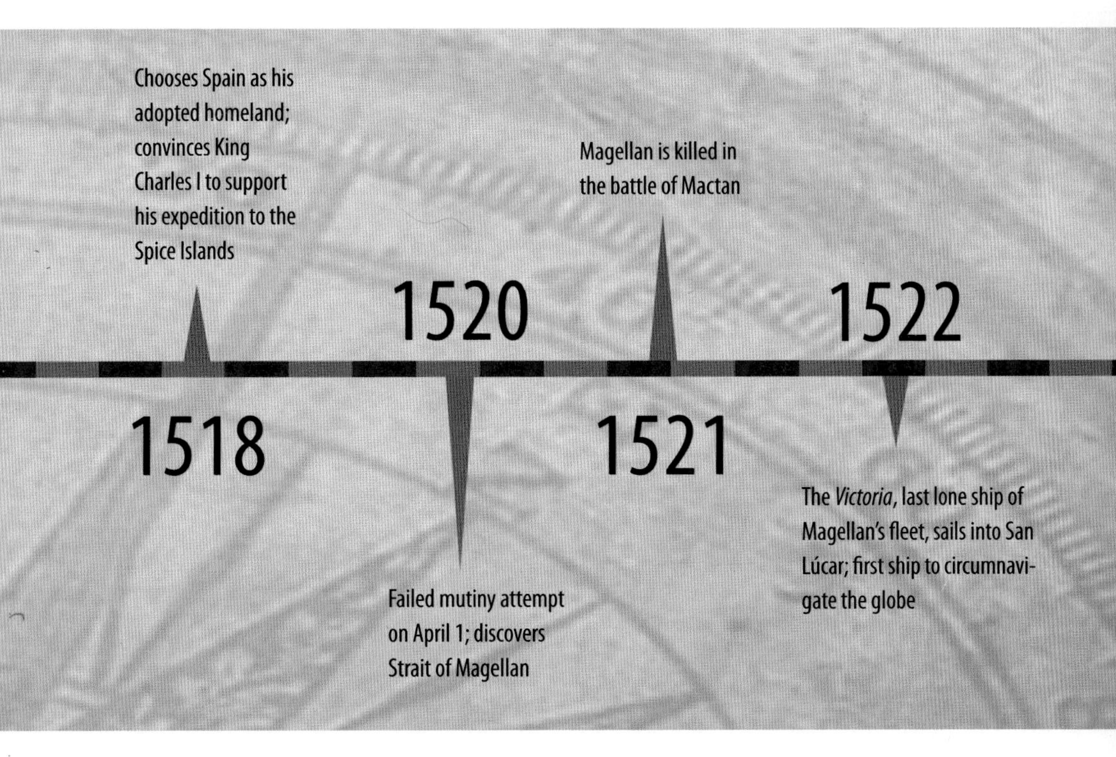

1518	Leaves Portugal and chooses Spain as his adopted homeland; convinces young King Charles I of Spain to support his expedition to the Spice Islands.
1519	Moloccan Fleet sets sail from San Lúcar on September 20.
1520	Moluccan Fleet winters at San Julián in southern Argentina; a failed mutiny attempt erupts on Easter, April 1; on October 21, the fleet discovers the Strait of Magellan, which leads the ships to the Pacific Ocean on November 25; the *San Antonio* mutinies and sails back to Spain.
1521	Magellan's fleet sails the Pacific Ocean, reaches the Pacific island of Guam on March 6; on March 16, Magellan discovers the Philippines, Magellan is killed at the battle of Mactan on April 27. The expedition splits, with the *Victoria* and the *Trinidad* sailing separately.
1522	Portuguese ships capture the *Trinidad*. The last lone ship of Magellan's fleet—the *Victoria*—sails into San Lúcar, Spain, on September 6 with only 18 European survivors, becoming the first ship to ever circumnavigate the globe.

Glossary

Abreast side by side

Ballast heavy material that is placed in the hold of a ship to give it stability

Bilges the lowest inner part of a ship's hull

Careen to turn a ship on its side for cleaning, caulking, or repairing

Cartographer someone who creates maps or charts

Cavalry troops trained to fight on horseback

Circumnavigate; circumnavigation to go completely around

Doldrums a region of the ocean near the equator, characterized by calms, light winds, or squalls

Dowry money or property offered to a potential husband by the bride's family

Estuary an arm of the sea that extends inland where it meets the mouth of a river

Farol a lantern

Forecastles the section of the upper deck of a ship located at the bow

Garrison a military post, especially one that is permanently established

Gunner cannon

Hull the frame or body of a ship

INSOLENT rude or disrespectful

JUNK a Chinese flatbottom ship

LEAGUE a unit of distance equal to three miles

MAROON to abandon on a deserted island where there is little hope of rescue or escape

MASTHEAD the top of the mast, which is the vertical pole that holds a ship's sail

MONASTERY a community of people, especially monks, bound by vows to a religious life, often living in partial or complete seclusion

MONOPOLY exclusive control by one group over a commodity or service

OUTRIGGER CANOE a canoe with a beam that extends out to one side to which the corner of a sail is tied

PAGE a youth employed by the royal court

PIROGUE a canoe made from a hollow tree trunk

PROBES expeditions of exploration

RECONNAISSANCE inspection of an area

REEF a ridge of rocks, sand, or coral that makes the water dangerously shallow for ships

RESOLUTION a formal statement of a group

SAMPAN a flat-bottomed boat used in Asia

SARONG a garment consisting of a long strip of printed cloth wrapped about the waist that is worn by men and women in Malaysia, Indonesia, and the Pacific islands

SCUTTLE to sink a ship by knocking holes in the hull

SHALLOP a small open boat fitted with oars or sails, or both, and used primarily in shallow waters

SHOAL a sandbar that makes the water shallow

SKIFF a flatbottom open boat with oars

SPOILS goods or property seized from the enemy after a victory

SQUALL a brief sudden violent windstorm, often accompanied by rain or snow

STERNCASTLE the rear end of a sailing ship, also known as the aftercastle

STOCKS a device used in punishment consisting of a heavy wooden frame with holes in which the feet, hands, and/or head of an offender can be locked

TEMPEST a violent storm

TRIBUTARIES streams that flow into larger streams, rivers, or a body of water

TRIBUTE a gift or payment

YARDARM a long horizontal pole tapered at the end and used to support and spread a square sail

BIBLIOGRAPHY

Bergreen, Laurence. *Over the Edge of the World.* New York: William Morrow, 2003.

Guillemard, F.H.H. *The Life of Ferdinand Magellan and the First Circumnavigation of the Globe.* New York: AMS Press, 1971.

Hawthorne, Daniel. *Ferdinand Magellan: The Biography of the Explorer Who First Showed the Way around the World.* Garden City, N.Y.: Doubleday & Company, Inc., 1964.

Joyner, Tim. *Magellan.* Camden, Maine: International Marine, 1992.

Nowell, Charles E., Ed. *Magellan's Voyage Around the World: Three Contemporary Accounts.* Evanston, Ill.: Northwestern University Press, 1962.

Parr, Charles McKew. *Ferdinand Magellan, Circumnavigator.* New York: Thomas Y. Crowell Company, 1964.

Roditi, Edouard. *Magellan of the Pacific.* New York: McGraw-Hill Book Company, 1972.

Sanderlin, George. *First Around the World: A Journal of Magellan's Voyage.* New York: Harper & Row Publishers, 1964.

Further Resources

Kramer, S. A. *Who Was Ferdinand Magellan?* New York: Grosset and Dunlap, 2004.

Lace, William W. *Captain James Cook*. New York: Chelsea House Publishers, 2009.

Levinson, Nancy Smiler. *Magellan and the First Voyage around the World*. New York: Clarion Books, 2001.

Pigafetta, Antonio, et. al. *Magellan*. UK: Viartis, 2008.

Velho, Alvaro, e. al. *Bartholomew Diaz*. UK: Viartis, 2008.

Wagner, Heather Lehr. *Hernán Cortés*. New York: Chelsea House Publishers, 2009.

Worth, Richard. *Vasco da Gama*. New York: Chelsea House Publishers, 2009.

WEB SITES

The European Voyages of Exploration

http://www.ucalgary.ca/applied_history/tutor/eurvoya/portuguese.html

Site that examines in detail the motivations, actions, and consequences of Portuguese and Spanish exploration in the fifteenth and sixteenth centuries.

The Mariners Museum

http://www.mariner.org

The online library for one of the largest international maritime history museums.

Sea and Sky: Explore the Skies Above and the Seas Below

http://www.seasky.org/index.html

Award-winning site dedicated to sharing information about the oceans and the wonders of the universe.

Seven Oceans

http://www.sevenoceans.com

Dedicated to maritime subjects like sailing, pirates, circumnavigation, ocean racing.

PICTURE CREDITS

PAGE

7: North Wind Pictures/ Photolibrary
13: © Infobase Publishing
17: Bildarchiv Preussischer Kulturbesitz/Art Resource, NY
23: British Library, London, UK /The Bridgeman Art Library
30: © INTERFOTO Pressebildagentur/Alamy
41: © North Wind Picture Archives/Alamy
47: © Look and Learn/ The Bridgeman Art Library
50: Aaron McCoy/ Photolibrary
60: © Stefano Bianchetti/ Corbis
66: © Infobase Publishing
70: © Ken Gillam/Robert Harding Picture Library/ Agefotostock
74: © Look and Learn/The Bridgeman Art Library
81: © Dave G. Houser/ Corbis
85: © Look and Learn/ The Bridgeman Art Library
94: Erich Lessing/Art Resource, NY
96: Hulton Archive/ Getty Images

INDEX

T

U

V

W

Z

About the Author

RACHEL A. KOESTLER-GRACK has worked with nonfiction books as an editor and writer since 1999. During her career, she has worked extensively with historical topics, ranging from the Middle Ages to the colonial era to the civil rights movement. In addition, she has written numerous biographies on a variety of historical and contemporary figures. Rachel lives with her husband and daughter in the German community of New Ulm, Minnesota.